W9-CDG-051

PAPER DINOSAURS

David Hawcock

Sterling Publishing Co., Inc.   New York

j 745.592
H 389 pap
c.1

House Editor: Donna Wood
Editor: Aidan Walker
Art Editor: Chris Walker
Photography: Ray Duns
Illustrations: John Hutchinson
Production: Craig Chubb

Published by Sterling Publishing Co, Inc.
Two Park Avenue, New York, N.Y. 10016

This book may not be sold outside the United States
of America and Canada with the exception of the
Coles chain of stores.

© Marshall Cavendish Limited 1988

ISBN 0−8069−6890−7 (paperback)
0−8069−6891−5 (hardback)

All rights reserved.

No part of this publication may be reproduced, stored in a
retrieval system or transmitted, in any form or by any means,
electronic, mechanical, photocopying, recording or otherwise,
without the prior permission of the copyright holders.

Typeset in 10/11pt Triumvirate by Quadraset Limited

Printed and bound in Spain

HEIGHTS PUBLIC LIBRARY

CONTENTS

INTRODUCTION

The dual components of this book – dinosaurs and paper – seem strangely incongruous. What has each got to do with either? But start to leaf through the pages, and if you like making things, you'll become fascinated . . . absorbed . . . and in no time find yourself eager to embark on this collection of challenging and amusing projects.

More and more people, not just children, are turning into dinosaur fanatics. It's nothing new: Richard Owen, a British anatomist, first coined the word in 1841. It is a combination of the Greek *deinos* and *sauros*, and means 'terrible reptile'. Owen's researches into the few available fossil remains at that time led him to conclude that three large animals – *Iguanadon*, *Megalosaurus* and *Hylaeosaurus* – were different from any other known animal types, either alive or long, long dead. They had the form of reptiles, but they were akin to elephants in size, and, most important, their legs were 'straight up and down' underneath their bodies, instead of spread out each side like those of other reptiles. They could walk and run, was the theory, far farther, faster, and more efficiently than their 'ordinary' reptilian relatives. These creatures Owen classified as Dinosaurs.

Dinosaurs populate an enduring world of fantasy and imagination amongst children, and are equally the subject of fascination, even obsession, with scientists, who have researched an enormous body of systematic knowledge about them. But these bizarre monsters have a hold on the imagination of us all; whenever a new dinosaur 'find' is announced, TV and newspapers, both popular and serious, make it big news. Friendly or terrible, playful or vengeful, they seem to personify forces of myth and magic which stir our collective psyche. Whether we emerged, like them, from the primeval slime, or popped into the world as fully-fledged humans, dinosaurs are a link for us with our own pre-history.

Strictly speaking, 'dinosaur' is a term that applies to a surprisingly limited group. They are technically confined to a particular period – the Mesozoic, which lasted from about 225 million to 64 million years ago; they were specifically land-living reptiles, with definite leg and hip bone structures (*saurischian*, reptile-hipped, or *ornithschian*, bird-hipped). Thus many of the creatures in this book are not technically dinosaurs at all; neither pterodactyls nor plesiosaurs, for instance, airborne and sea-living, qualify for the name. These, like dinosaurs, are part of a larger group known as 'archosaurs', ruling reptiles. So perhaps the book should be called 'Paper Prehistoric Animals' – some of the animals you will be making were not even archosaurs. But 'Dinosaur' is the name we know, the one that fires the imagination.

USING PAPER

If you are familiar neither with dinosaurs nor with paper as a modelling material, you have a double treat in store. Paper is remarkably versatile and rewarding stuff to make things with; it's inexpensive and easily available, you get quick results, and once you're used to handling and gluing it, it will behave exactly as you want. It's encouragingly easy, and to create the models in this book you do not need expensive equipment. A good craft knife or scalpel, a pair of scissors, glue and perhaps a few paperclips to hold newly glued parts together, or some adhesive tape are all you require.

Paper comes in a staggering variety of colours, textures, sizes and weights, from which you must choose for each project. (You will become a valued customer of your local art shop!) The photographs of the animals show the many different colours available, but there is no need to stick to these guidelines – you can follow your own inspiration.

Weight: Follow the recommendations at the start of each project until you become confident enough to make your own decisions. All of the models in this book are made from either thin, medium or thick paper. What we refer to as 'thin' is heavy typing paper weight, 'medium' is the weight of what is known as ledger or construction paper in the US, cartridge paper in the UK, and 'thick' is known in the US as card stock and in the UK as ticket card. For UK readers, 'thin'=80gsm, 'medium'=100gsm and 'thick'=200gsm.

Use the right weight for the right job. Don't try to make small intricate shapes with thick card, and likewise don't expect a monster to stand up if you make its structural pieces with very thin paper. Shiny metallic paper almost always comes thin, so you will have to back it by gluing a heavier sheet of paper to it.

Sizes: There is an ISO (International Standards Organisation) system for paper sizes in the UK and Europe. This is the rectangular series, in which A0, the largest, is twice the area of A1, which is twice the area of A2, and so on down to the smallest size, A10. (To give you an idea, a standard paperback book would be A5, while the commonest magazine size is A4.) The idea is that the ratio of length to width is always the same, so the proportions will always be the same whatever the size. A diagram that fits A0 will reduce proportionally to fit A4, A7, or any other size in the series. In the US, however, there is no standardized sizing system, so sheets of paper will have to be ordered individually to size.

Tools: You will always need a pair of good sharp scissors for cutting out large pieces, and a scalpel or craft knife for smaller, more intricate cuts. It's best to have 'paper only' scissors and a knife with replaceable blades, as paper is surprisingly abrasive, and can blunt tools quite quickly. Other requirements are noted at the beginning of each project in the 'You will need' list.

TERMS USED IN THE INSTRUCTIONS

There are a few standard techniques you should know about when modelling in paper:

Scoring: Making a line with the blade of the knife or scissors (or the back of either, if you don't want it too sharply defined) so you can control the exact line of a fold. This is used almost as much as cutting. If you use the blade, you must develop a light 'touch' so you do not cut right through.

Lining: Backing one paper with another. This is used mainly in the projects in this book for mouths, but other animals will have the

Paper Size Conversion Chart

Within this book, only four different sizes of paper in the ISO series have been used; SRA2, A2, A3 and A4. This chart provides a conversion table for metric and standard equivalents, to enable you to buy the right quantity of paper for each project:

Standard	US Equivalents	Metric	
17¾ × 25¼in	18 × 24in	450 × 640mm	SRA2
16½ × 23⅜in	18 × 24in	420 × 594mm	, A2
11¾ × 16½in	12 × 18in	297 × 420mm	A3
8¼ × 11¾in	9 × 12in	210 × 297mm	A4

Paper sizes provided by Wiggins Teape

insides of ears and perhaps eye cavities different colours. Just glue two sheets together and use them as one, remembering that their weight will combine. When you have folded and made a cut, the inside of the shape will show the lining colour.

Creasing: Pinching a piece to help it keep shape, alter the shape, or give an expression to a face or mouth.

USING THE DRAWINGS

For each monster there are two sets of drawings, one on grids which you can scale up and cut full-size shapes from, the other a more three-dimensional representation which shows how the pieces fit together. On the 'flat' gridded drawings, glue numbered parts to parts with the same number. The tones and markings on the drawings tell you whether you should apply glue to the top or the underside of an area. A line made up of dots and dashes tells you that only half a part appears on the drawing, the other half of which is a mirror image, so it can be drawn and cut out of a piece of paper folded double. Of course in such cases only one set of numbers will appear, so you have to

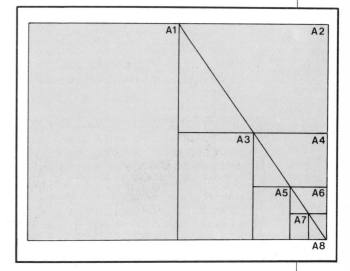

imagine their counterparts and just glue the pieces together symmetrically.

Start with an easy model, then move on to the more challenging ones, then you can branch out and create a whole new species of your own mysterious, mythical monsters.

Above all, have fun!

TYRANNOSAURUS REX

When you say 'Dinosaur' to someone who is neither a fanatic nor a connoisseur, *Tyrannosaurus Rex* ('Tyrant reptile') is the animal they'll think of. Members of this species were the largest known carnivores, reaching 46ft (14m) in length and 7 tons in weight. They are both terrifying and ridiculous in appearance, with their enormous heads, fiercesome teeth and powerful hind limbs, yet their forelimbs are so small as to be pathetic. There is a theory that the forelimbs were used as 'brakes' when the animal rose to an upright position; it would straighten its huge rear legs first, and so needed some kind of hold to stop its nose being pushed along the ground!

YOU WILL NEED
Scalpel or modelling knife
Scissors
Impact adhesive

3 sheets of minimum 16½×23⅜in (420×594mm) thick orange paper
1 sheet of minimum 16½×23⅜in (420×594mm) thick yellow paper
1 sheet of minimum 11¾×16½in (297×420mm) thick white paper
1 sheet of minimum 11¾×16½in (297×420mm) thick pink paper
Offcuts of red paper

1 Cut out both sides of the body from orange paper. Join A to **A**.

2 Cut out the belly from yellow paper.

3 Glue the body sides together along the back at 1 to **1**.

4 Glue the belly into position 2 to **2**.

5 Cut out the three tail pieces – the two sides from orange paper, the underside from yellow paper.

6 Glue the two sides of the tail together 3 to **3**. Glue the tail underside into position 5 to **5** and 4 to **4**.

7 Glue the tail to the body 6 to **6** and 7 to **7**.

8 Cut out the neck from orange paper.

9 Glue 8 to **8** to make the neck.

10 Glue the neck to the body 9 to **9**, 10 to **10** and 11 to **11**.

11 Glue 12 to **12** on the upper leg. Glue 13 to **13** on the lower leg. Glue 14 to **14** on the lower leg.

12 Join the upper and lower legs together, 15 to **15**.

13 Insert the knee 16 to **16**.

14 Fold up the foot, gluing both sides of the 'crimp': 17 to **17** and 18 to **18**, then 19 to **19**, 20 to **20** and 21 to **21**. Finally fold it right round to get the main shape, 22 to **22**.

15 Attach the foot to the leg, 24 to **24** and 23 to **23**.

16 Repeat steps 11–16 using mirror image pieces for the second leg.

17 Attach the leg to the body, 25 to **25**.

18 Repeat the stages for the second leg on the opposite side.

19 Cut out an upper and lower arm.

20 Glue 26 to **26** on the upper arm and 27 to **27** on the lower arm.

21 Join the upper and lower arm together 28 to **28**.

22 Join the arm to the body, 29 to **29**.

23 Repeat steps 20–23 using mirror image pieces for the second arm.

24 Cut out the upper jaw. Glue 30 to **30** and 31 to **31**.

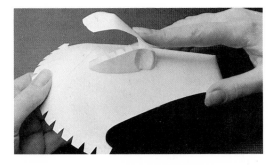

Assembling the eyes and the top of the model's head.

25 Cut out the lower jaw. Glue 32 to **32** and 33 to **33**.

26 Cut out the upper palate, remembering to cut the slots.

27 Glue the upper palate into position in the upper jaw, 34 to **34**.

28 Cut out the lower palate in the same way, and glue it into position in the lower jaw, 35 to **35**.

29 Join together the upper and lower jaws 36 to **36**.

30 Cut out the teeth from white paper. Slot tabs B into slots **B** on the upper jaw and tabs C into slots **C** in the lower jaw.

31 Cut out the forehead and two eyes. Paint the eye areas to give the model some expression.

32 Join 37 to **37** on the forehead.

33 Fold up each eye 38 to **38** and 39 to **39**.

34 Glue each eye into place on the forehead, 40 to **40** and 41 to **41**.

35 Glue the eye/forehead assembly into position on the upper jaw. Tab A goes into slot A: glue 42 to **42** and 43 to **43**.

36 Finally, glue the head on to the neck 44 to **44**, 45 to **45**.

37 To enhance the completed model, cut out six white claws. Glue 46 to **46** and 47 to **47**.

38 Glue a claw into each toe.

39 Cut out the tongue from red paper and position it in the model's mouth.

TYRANNOSAURUS REX

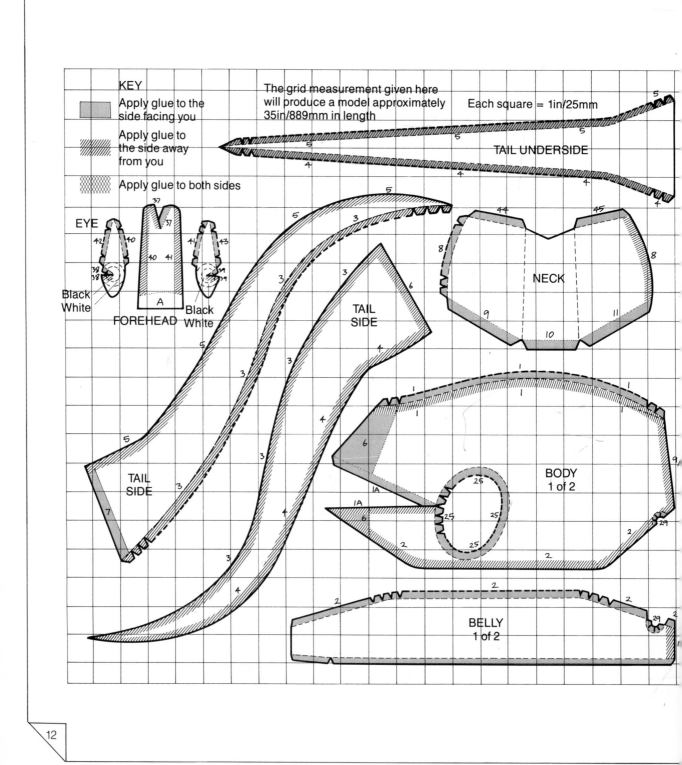

KEY

Apply glue to the side facing you

Apply glue to the side away from you

Apply glue to both sides

The grid measurement given here will produce a model approximately 35in/889mm in length

Each square = 1in/25mm

TAIL UNDERSIDE

EYE

FOREHEAD

Black White

Black White

A

NECK

TAIL SIDE

TAIL SIDE

BODY 1 of 2

BELLY 1 of 2

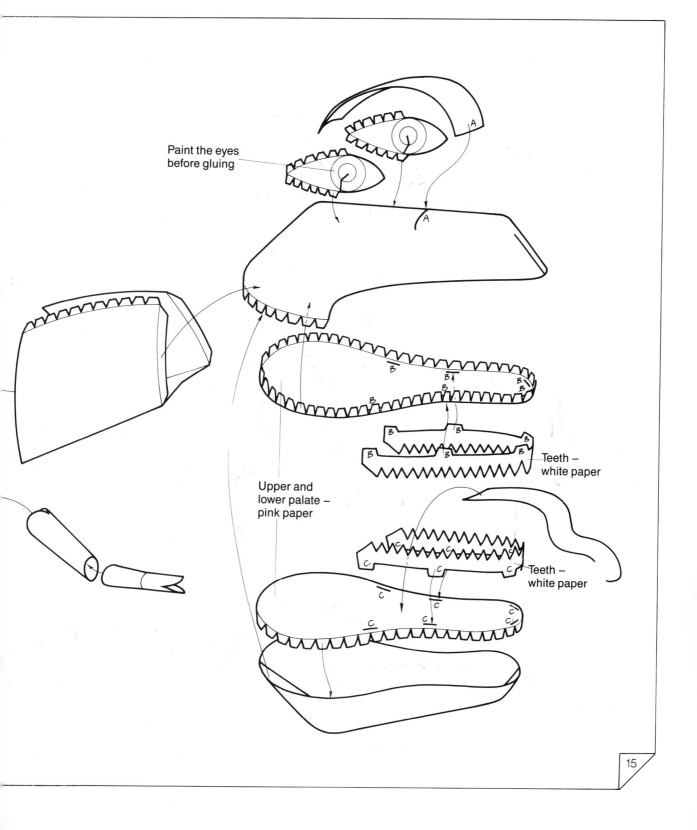

Paint the eyes
before gluing

Upper and
lower palate –
pink paper

Teeth –
white paper

Teeth –
white paper

PARASAUROLOPHUS

Parasaurolophus ('Beside ridged reptile') was a member of the Hadrosaurid family, amongst the 'youngest' of dinosaur groups, which have been placed at the end of the Cretaceous period – a mere 80–64 million years ago. They were mild-mannered vegetarians, and suggestions have been made that they lived mainly on or near water; though it's doubtful that they were actually amphibious, their large tails and feet indicate that they would have been good swimmers.

Hadrosaurids divide into two groups, those with weird head crests – like *Parasaurolophus*, whose crest at up to 3.3ft (1m) is the longest known – and those with duck-like bills. Their anatomy, apart from the skull variations, follows a fairly common *Iguanadon*-like plan; large bodies and hind legs, large tails, smaller front limbs.

YOU WILL NEED
Scalpel or modelling knife
Scissors
Impact adhesive

1 sheet of minimum 16½ × 23⅜in (420 × 594mm) thick yellow paper
3 sheets of minimum 16½ × 23⅜in (420 × 594mm) thick purple paper
1 sheet of minimum 11¾ × 16½in (297 × 420mm) thick white paper
1 sheet of minimum 16½ × 23⅜in (420 × 594mm) thin yellow paper
1 sheet of minimum 8¼ × 11¾in (210 × 297mm) thick pink paper
Offcuts of red paper

1 Make the body in the same way as *Tyrannosaurus Rex* (see page 8).

2 Make the arms in the same way as *Tyrannosaurus Rex* and stick these to the body.

3 Cut out the three pieces that make up a leg and also a foot from purple paper.

4 On the upper leg glue 1 to **1**.

5 On the lower leg glue 2 to **2**.

6 Join the upper and lower legs 3 to **3**.

7 Insert the knee 4 to **4**.

8 Fold up the foot and glue 5 to **5**, 6 to **6**, 7 to **7**, 8 to **8**, 9 to **9** and finally 10 to **10**.

9 Stick the complete foot to the base of the leg, 11 to **11** and 12 to **12**.

10 Stick the complete leg into the body. Cut out the white claws, fold and glue them and stick them in the foot, 13 to **13**.

11 Repeat steps 3–10 for the second leg, using mirror image pieces.

12 Cut out the two tail sides from purple paper and the tail base from thick yellow paper.

13 Glue side A to the tail base, 14 to **14**.

14 Glue side B to the base, 15 to **15** and to side A, 16 to **16**.

15 Glue the complete tail to the body: the *Tyrannosaurus Rex* parts are numbered 6 and 7 in that project. Here parts **17**, **18** and **19** glue to the equivalent areas on the *Parasaurolophus* body.

16 Cut out two neck sides from purple paper and one neck front from thick yellow paper.

17 Glue the two neck sides together, 20 to **20**.

18 Insert the neck front and glue 21 to **21** and 22 to **22**.

19 Glue parts **23**, 24, and 25 of the neck into the body.

20 Cut out the five pieces that form the head top and the two jowls from purple paper. Cut out the upper jaw from pink paper.

21 Glue 26 to **26** and 27 to **27**, positioning the brow.

22 Form the snout by gluing 28 to **28**, and the back of the head 29 to **29**.

23 Cut out the upper jaw from thick pink paper. Insert the upper jaw into the head, 30 to **30**.

24 Glue the jowls into position, 31 to **31**.

25 Cut out the lower head from purple paper.

26 Glue 32 to **32** and 33 to **33**.

27 Cut out the lower jaw from thick pink paper. Insert it into the head and glue 34 to **34**.

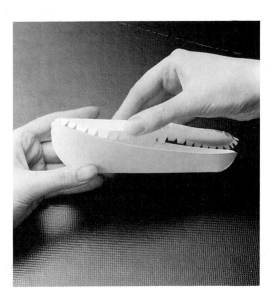

Assembling the lower jaw. The rows of tabs are stuck in place.

28 Join the upper and lower head pieces 35 to **35**.

29 Cut out the three pieces that make the crest from purple paper.

30 Glue 36 to **36**.

31 Glue 37 to **37** and 38 to **38**.

32 Glue the finished crest on to the top of the head, 39 to **39**.

33 Cut out two sets of white teeth. Glue them on to the jaws, 40 to **40**.

34 Attach a red tongue to the inside of the bottom jaw if you wish.

35 Cut out the yellow body patterns from the thin paper and stick them on the back of the model's head, body and tail.

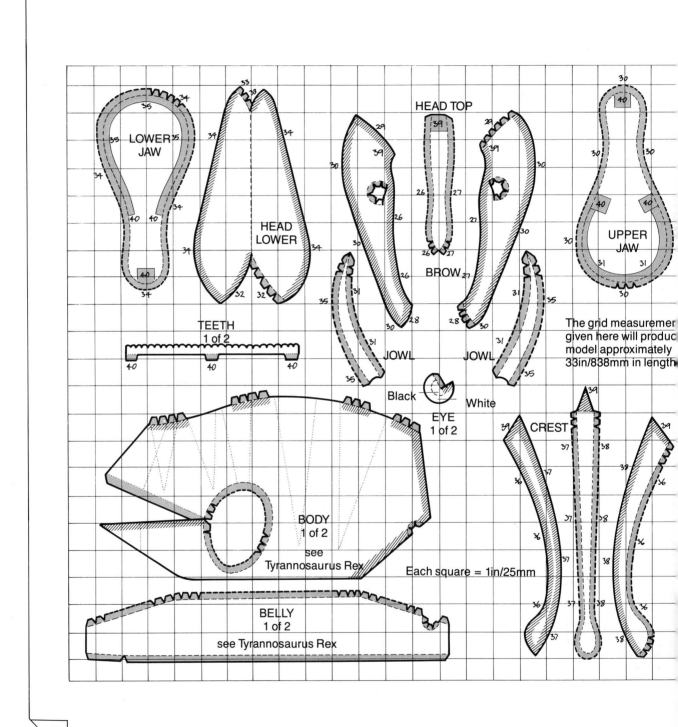

LOWER JAW

HEAD TOP

HEAD LOWER

BROW

UPPER JAW

TEETH
1 of 2

JOWL

JOWL

The grid measuremer given here will produc model approximately 33in/838mm in length

Black

White

EYE
1 of 2

CREST

BODY
1 of 2

see
Tyrannosaurus Rex

Each square = 1in/25mm

BELLY
1 of 2

see Tyrannosaurus Rex

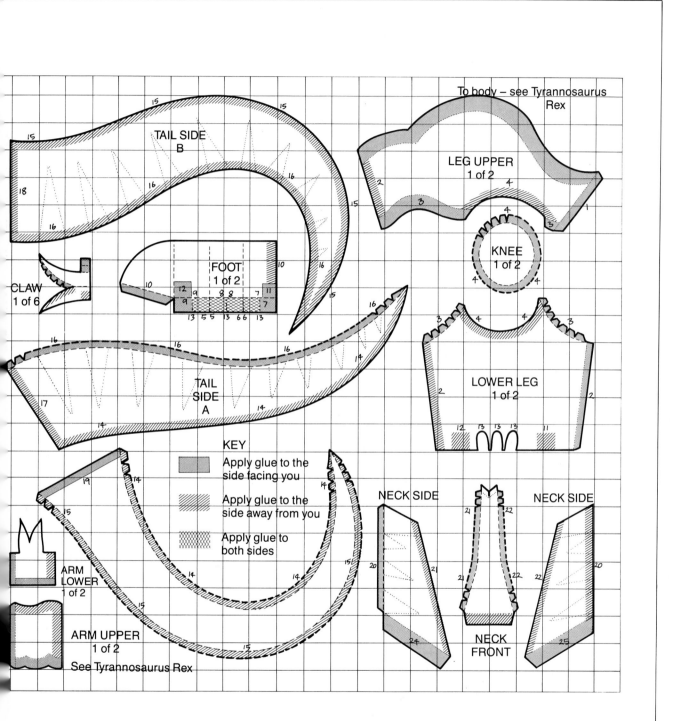

To body – see Tyrannosaurus Rex

TAIL SIDE B

LEG UPPER 1 of 2

CLAW 1 of 6

FOOT 1 of 2

KNEE 1 of 2

TAIL SIDE A

LOWER LEG 1 of 2

KEY

Apply glue to the side facing you

Apply glue to the side away from you

Apply glue to both sides

NECK SIDE

NECK SIDE

ARM LOWER 1 of 2

ARM UPPER 1 of 2
See Tyrannosaurus Rex

NECK FRONT

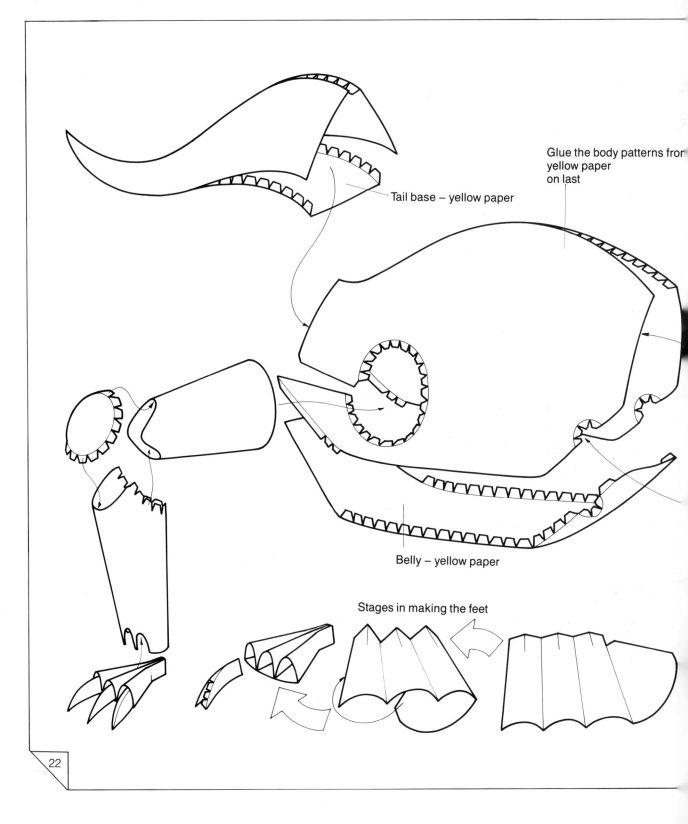

Tail base – yellow paper

Glue the body patterns from
yellow paper
on last

Belly – yellow paper

Stages in making the feet

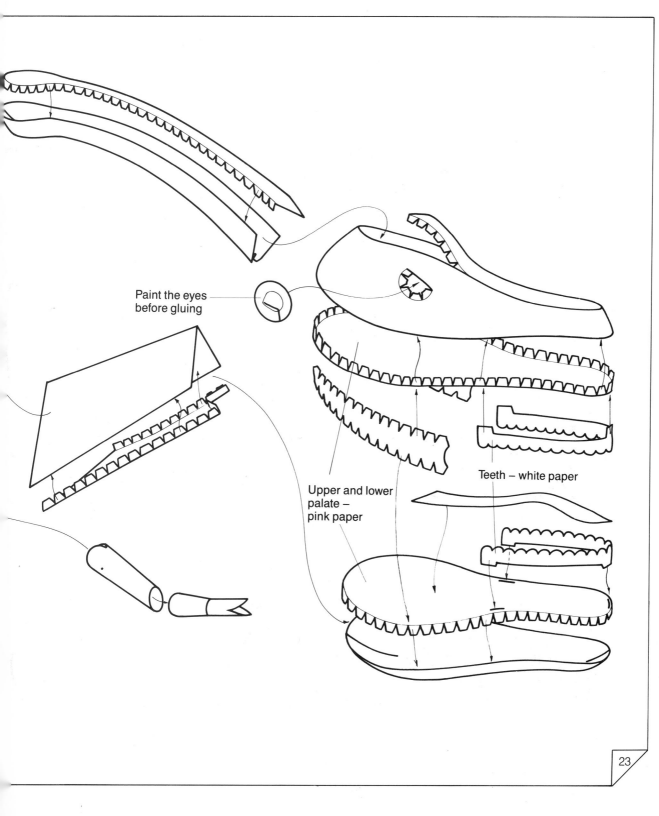

Paint the eyes
before gluing

Upper and lower
palate –
pink paper

Teeth – white paper

TRICERATOPS ALTICORNIS

Triceratops, a member of the Ceratopid family, is another of those 'essentially dinosaur' dinosaurs whose typical rhinoceros-like appearance is familiar to many others than scientists and enthusiasts. First discoveries of the remains of these animals were made in 1855, but much more detailed information became available in 1872. A discovery in 1885 of horn cores led one scientist to conclude they were from a species of buffalo – he called it *Bison Alticornis*, high-horned buffalo – which, he thought, had only recently become extinct. The cores themselves were 3ft (90cm) long, which indicates that a fully-covered horn would have been massive. As for the buffalo idea, *Triceratops* reached 30ft (9m) long, 12ft (3.3m) high, and 5.4 tons, while a *Torosaurus* (bull reptile) has been discovered which has the largest head of any known animal – the skull was over 8ft (2.4m) long!

(See colour photograph at the top of page 38.)

YOU WILL NEED
Scalpel or modelling knife
Scissors
Impact adhesive

3 sheets of minimum 16½×23⅜in (420×594mm) thick green paper
1 sheet of minimum 16½×23⅜in (420×594mm) thick orange paper
1 sheet of minimum 11¾×16½in (297×420mm) thin pink paper
1 sheet of minimum 8¼×11¾in (210×297mm) thick white paper

1 Stick some thin pink paper to the underside of the green sheet so you can cut out the two sets of body halves, the top green and the bottom pink.

2 Glue 1 to **1**.

3 Glue 2 to **2**.

4 Glue 3 to **3**.

5 Glue 4 to **4**.

6 Cut out the three pieces that form the tail, the two sides from green paper and the underside from orange.

7 Glue 5 to **5**, then stick the tail underside in position, 6 to **6**, 7 to **7**.

8 Stick the tail into position on the body, 8 to **8**, 9 to **9**.

9 Cut out the dinosaur's neck. Glue 10 to **10** and 11 to **11**. Stick the neck to the body 12 to **12**.

10 Cut out the four pieces that form the front leg.

11 Glue 13 to **13** on the upper leg.

12 Glue 14 to **14** on the lower leg.

13 Join the upper and lower leg 15 to **15**.

14 Insert the knee 16 to **16**.

15 Stick 17 to **17** on the hoof.

16 Stick the hoof into position on the leg 18 to **18**.

17 Cut out the four pieces that form the back leg.

18 Stick 19 to **19** on the upper leg.

19 Glue 20 to **20** on the lower leg.

20 Join the upper and lower leg, 21 to **21**.

21 Insert the knee, 22 to **22**.

22 Glue 23 to **23** on the hoof.

23 Glue the hoof to the lower leg, 24 to **24**.

24 Stick the front leg into the body, 25 to **25**, and the back leg likewise, 26 to **26**.

25 Repeat instructions 10–24 for the other two legs.

26 Before cutting out the two halves of each of the two pieces that form the head (four in all), line the green paper you will be using with the light weight pink paper. Now cut out the pieces for the head.

27 Colour the eyes as indicated, to give your *Triceratops* some facial expression.

28 On head piece 1, glue 27 to **27** to form the eye.

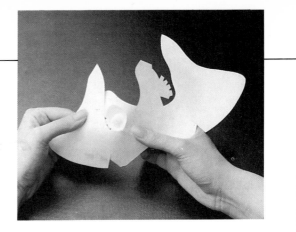

Forming the round, protruding shape of the eye.

29 Glue 28 to **28** to pull in the face.

30 Glue 29 to **29** and 30 to **30** to complete the shape of this half.

31 Repeat instructions 25–28 for the other half of head piece 1.

32 Glue 31 to **31** to form the complete top half of the head – piece 1.

33 Taking the two halves of head piece 2, glue 32 to **32**, 33 to **33**, and 34 to **34**.

34 Glue 35 to **35**. You now have a complete head piece 2.

35 Join the two head pieces 1 and 2 together by gluing points 36 to **36**.

36 Cut out the crest.

37 Stick it inside the complete head 37 to **37**.

38 Stick the complete head and crest assembly to the neck, 38 to **38**.

39 Make up the horns from white paper, 39 to **39** and 40 to **40**.

40 Glue the horns in position on the nose and above the eyes, 41 to **41** and 42 to **42**.

41 Cut out the toenails from white paper, and glue them to the hoofs 43 to **43**.

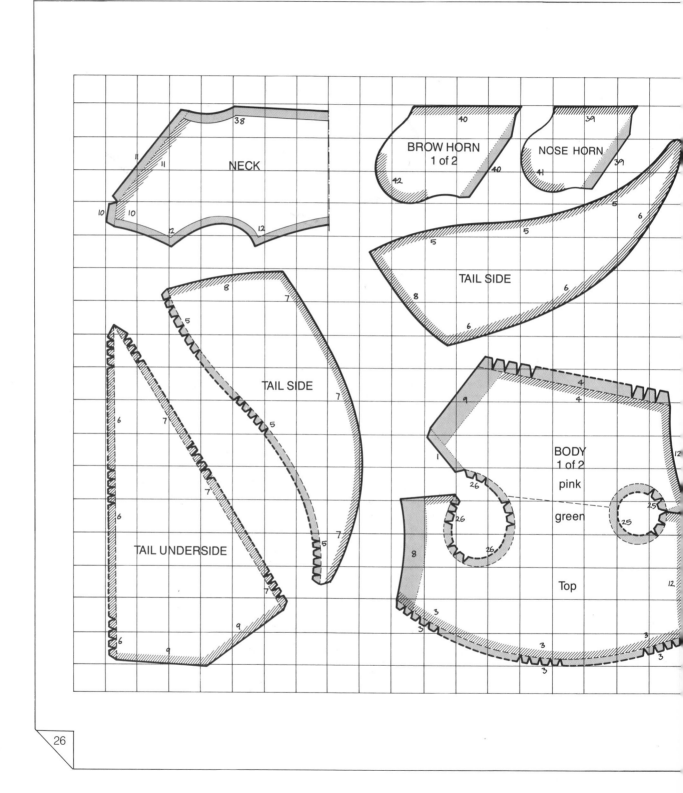

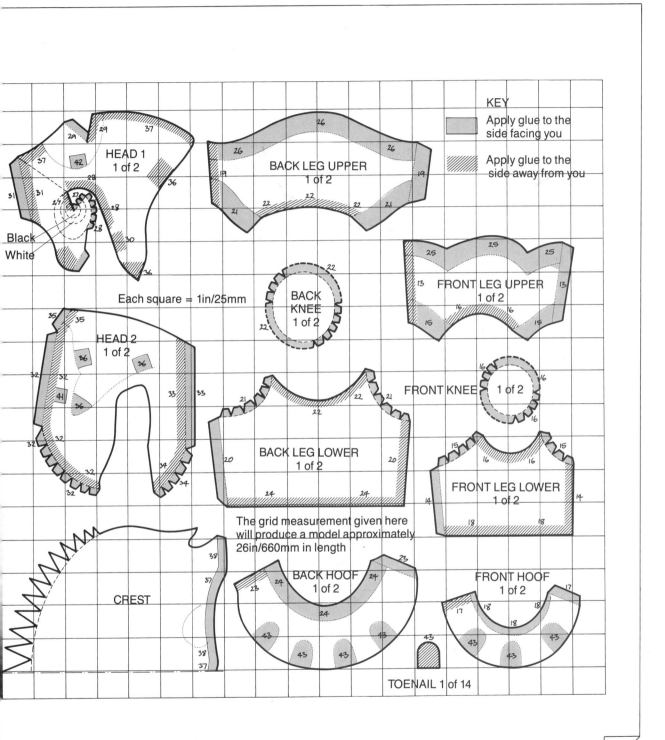

KEY

Apply glue to the side facing you

Apply glue to the side away from you

HEAD 1
1 of 2

Black
White

Each square = 1in/25mm

HEAD 2
1 of 2

BACK LEG UPPER
1 of 2

BACK
KNEE
1 of 2

FRONT LEG UPPER
1 of 2

FRONT KNEE   1 of 2

BACK LEG LOWER
1 of 2

FRONT LEG LOWER
1 of 2

The grid measurement given here
will produce a model approximately
26in/660mm in length

CREST

BACK HOOF
1 of 2

FRONT HOOF
1 of 2

TOENAIL 1 of 14

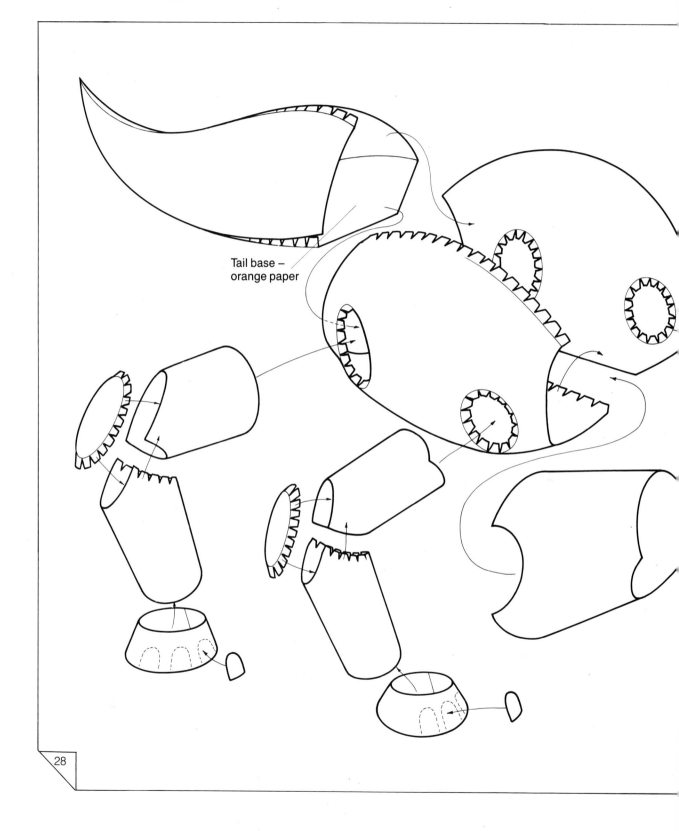

Tail base –
orange paper

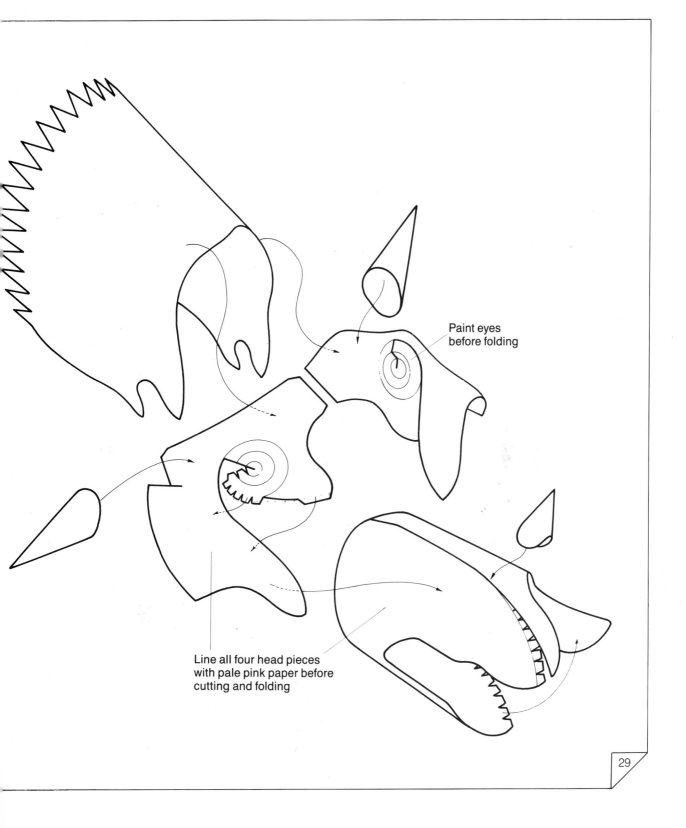

Paint eyes
before folding

Line all four head pieces
with pale pink paper before
cutting and folding

PTERODACTYLUS

This small flying reptile (small by some dinosaur standards), lived in the later Jurassic period, about 150 million years ago. Its remains have been found in lithographic limestone in Germany; it lived at the same time and in the same area as *Archaeopteryx*. *Pterodactylus* flew by flapping its wings – its wingspan was about 22in (56cm) – but it was slower moving and less efficient in its airborne movements than modern birds.

Impressions of fur have been found in the limestone, which as explained in the *Archaeopteryx* project is so fine that it keeps very detailed fossilized remains. This is why it was used for printing blocks – hence the name 'lithographic'. The *Pterodactylus*' fur suggests that they were warm-blooded, since one of the primary functions of a thick body covering like this is the prevention of heat loss.

Pterodactylus may have caught insects for food, or perhaps used its teeth to snatch small fish from the surface of the water.

(See colour photograph at the top of page 39.)

YOU WILL NEED
Scalpel or modelling knife
Scissors
Impact adhesive

1 sheet of minimum 11¾×16½in (297×420mm) thick buff paper
1 sheet of minimum 11¾×16½in (297×420mm) thick mid brown paper
1 sheet of minimum 11¾×16½in (297×420mm) thick dark brown paper
1 sheet of minimum 16½×23⅜in (420×594mm) thick marbled paper
1 sheet of minimum 8¼×11¾in (210×297mm) thick white paper
1 sheet of minimum 8¼×11¾in (210×297mm) thin pink paper

1 Cut out the body from buff paper.

2 Glue 1 to **1** and 2 to **2**.

3 Glue 3 to **3**.

4 Cut out the five pieces that form the neck from dark brown paper.

5 On piece 1 glue 4 to **4** to form a ring.

6 Likewise, on piece 2 glue 5 to **5**. Join piece 1 to 2 by gluing 6 to **6**.

7 On piece 3, glue 7 to **7**. Join piece 2 to pieces 1 and 2 by gluing 8 to **8**.

8 Glue 9 to **9** on piece 4 and join piece 4 to pieces 1, 2 and 3 by gluing 10 to **10**.

9 Glue 11 to **11** on piece 5. Join piece 5 to the rest of the neck by gluing 12 to **12**.

10 Glue the neck to the body, 13 to **13**.

11 Cut out the wings from marbled paper. Glue them to the body, 14 to **14**, 15 to **15**, 16 to **16** and 17 to **17**.

12 Cut out the two pieces that form an arm from buff paper.

13 Glue 18 to **18** on the upper arm and 19 to **19** on the lower arm.

14 Join the upper and lower arm, 20 to **20**.

15 Stick the arm into position on the wing, 21 to **21**.

16 Repeat steps 12–15 with mirror image pieces to form the second arm.

17 Cut out a leg from buff paper.

18 Glue 22 to **22**.

19 Stick it into position to the body and wing, 23 to **23**. Repeat this for the second leg.

20 Before cutting out the head from dark brown paper and the hands and feet from buff, stick a thin pink paper backing on to the pieces from which you will cut.

21 Cut out the two pieces that form the head.

22 Glue 24 to **24** and 25 to **25** on the upper head.

23 Glue 26 to **26** and 27 to **27** on the lower head.

24 Join the upper and lower head, 28 to **28**.

25 Glue the head on to the neck, 29 to **29**.

26 Cut out the hands and feet.

27 Glue the feet to the ends of the legs, 30 to **30**.

28 Glue the hands to the ends of the arms, 31 to **31**.

29 Cut out two eyes, each composed of a central blue spot, a white background and a yellow 'pupil'. Stick the eyes into position on the head.

30 Cut out the upper and lower teeth from white paper. Fold them in half and stick them in the mouth, 32 to **32**, 33 to **33**, on the upper jaw, and 34 to **34**, 35 to **35** in the lower jaw.

31 Cut out lots of strips of feathery hair from the two shades of brown paper, and starting at the tail, cover the animal's entire body with it in overlapping strips of alternate shades, as shown in the photograph.

The fur effect is achieved by building up the strips of fringed paper, starting at the back.

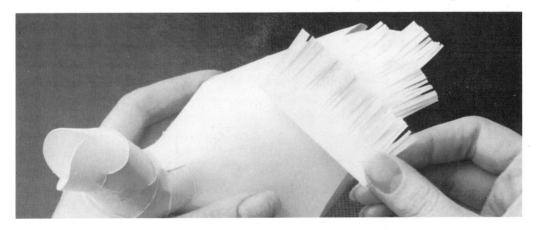

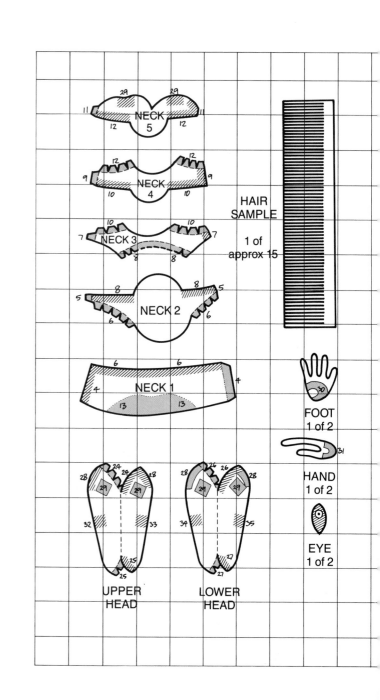

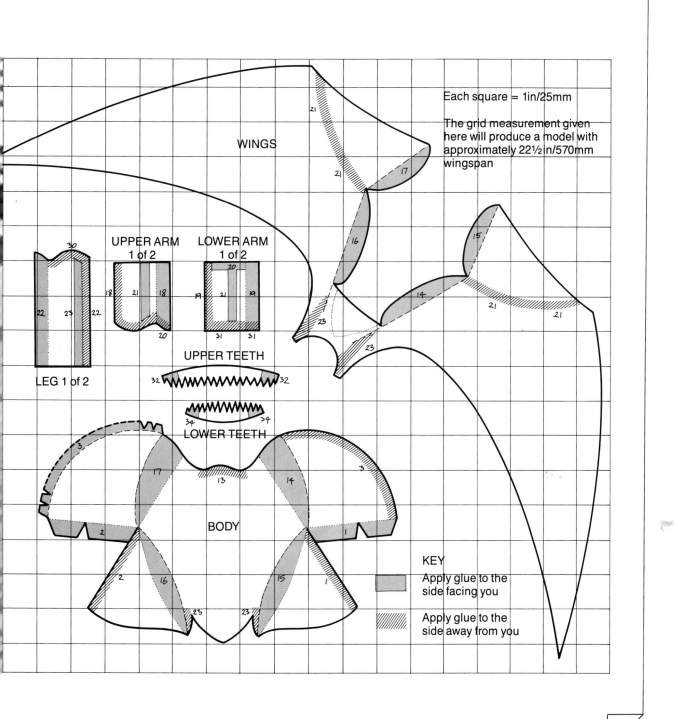

WINGS

Each square = 1in/25mm

The grid measurement given
here will produce a model with
approximately 22½in/570mm
wingspan

UPPER ARM
1 of 2

LOWER ARM
1 of 2

LEG 1 of 2

UPPER TEETH

LOWER TEETH

BODY

KEY

Apply glue to the
side facing you

Apply glue to the
side away from you

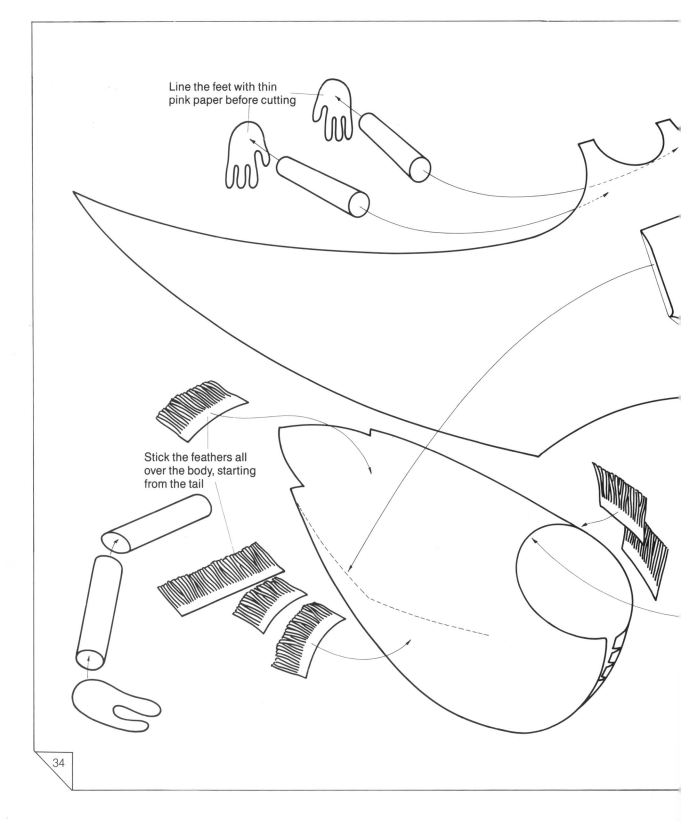

Line the feet with thin
pink paper before cutting

Stick the feathers all
over the body, starting
from the tail

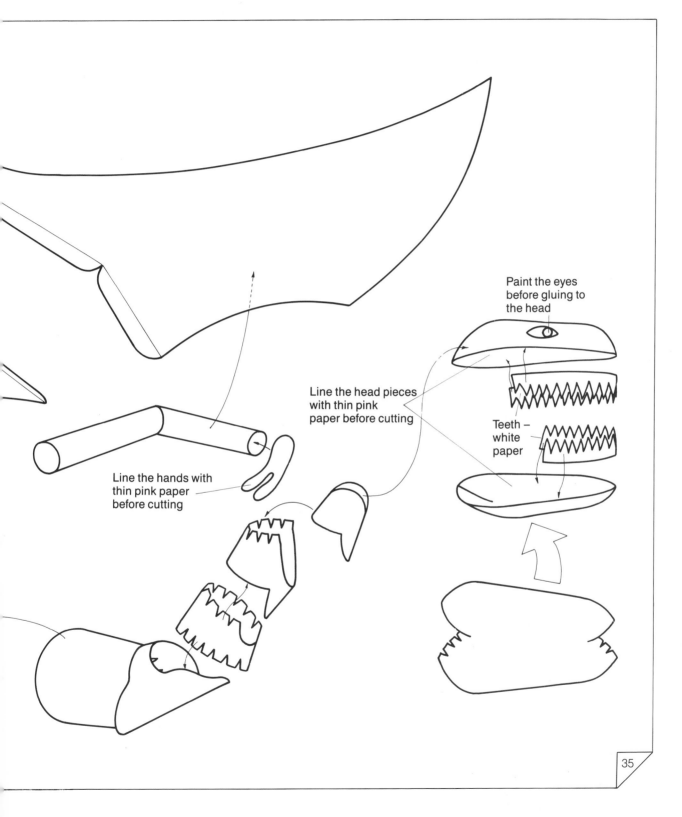

Paint the eyes
before gluing to
the head

Line the head pieces
with thin pink
paper before cutting

Teeth –
white
paper

Line the hands with
thin pink paper
before cutting

DINICHTHYS DUNKLEOSTEUS

Dinichthys was a member of the Placoderm family, a group of fish with a bony covering over the head and front part of the body. There was a movable joint between the two sets of armour, allowing the head to be moved and the mouth to be opened very wide. The jaws had no teeth, but their jagged edges would have allowed them to disable and destroy prey with ease. *Dinichthys* was the largest fish in this group, growing to over 30ft (9.14m) – longer than the Great White Shark, famous star of *Jaws*.

(See colour photograph on pages 38–39.)

YOU WILL NEED
Scalpel or modelling knife
Scissors
Impact adhesive

1 sheet of minimum 16½ × 23⅜in (420 × 594mm) thick red paper
1 sheet of minimum 16½ × 23⅜in (420 × 594mm) thick white paper
1 sheet of minimum 11¾ × 16½in (297 × 420mm) thick silver paper
1 sheet of minimum 11¾ × 16½in (297 × 420mm) thick brown paper

1 Cut out one body section from red paper and six pieces of facial patterning from silver. Glue the pattern to the body, 1 to **1**, 2 to **2**, 3 to **3**, 4 to **4**, 5 to **5**, and 6 to **6**.

2 Repeat this with mirror image pieces for the second half of the body.

3 Glue 7 to **7** on each body half.

4 Join the two halves of the body, 8 to **8**.

5 Cut out the belly from white paper.

6 Cut out two fins and two mirror image fins.

7 Glue the fins into place on the belly, 9 to **9**, 10 to **10**.

8 Glue the belly and fins to the body, 11 to **11**.

9 Glue 12 to **12** on the belly.

10 Colour the eyes as indicated in the photograph, fold up and glue 13 to **13**.

11 Stick the complete eyes into the sockets, 14 to **14**.

12 Cut out the upper and lower teeth and stick the upper teeth on to the body, inside the mouth, 15 to **15**.

13 Stick the lower teeth on to the belly, inside the mouth, 16 to **16**.

14 Cut out a dorsal fin from brown paper. Decorate it with thin strips of silver. Slot it into position along the back of the body, tab A to slot **A**.

15 Cut out a lower fin and slot it into the belly to finish the model, tab B to slot **B**.

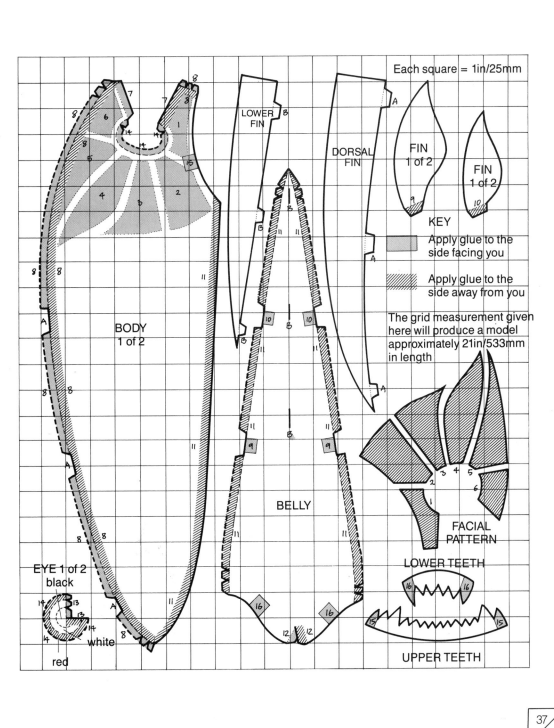

Each square = 1in/25mm

LOWER FIN

DORSAL FIN

FIN 1 of 2

FIN 1 of 2

KEY

Apply glue to the side facing you

Apply glue to the side away from you

The grid measurement given here will produce a model approximately 21in/533mm in length

BODY 1 of 2

BELLY

FACIAL PATTERN

LOWER TEETH

UPPER TEETH

EYE 1 of 2
black
white
red

Above: Triceratops Alticornis
Above right: Pterodactylus
Right: Dinichthys Dunkleosteus

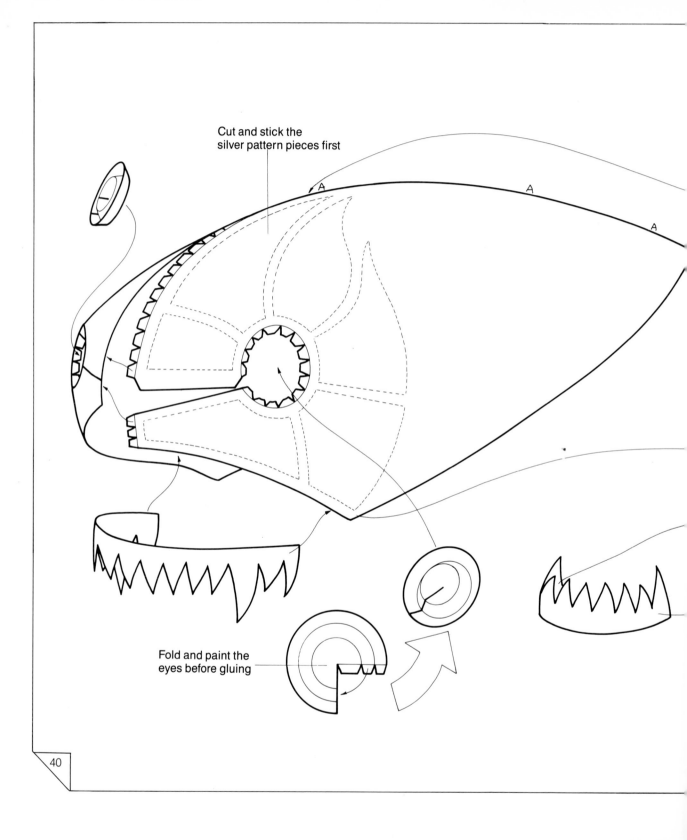

Cut and stick the
silver pattern pieces first

A

A

A

Fold and paint the
eyes before gluing

40

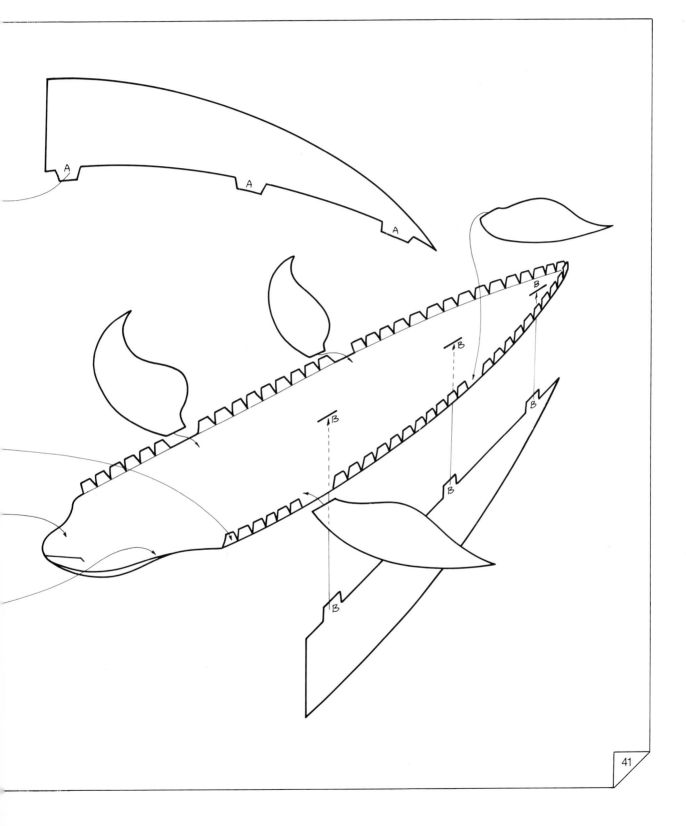

CRYPTOCLIDUS PLESIOSAUR

The Plesiosaur family, of which *Cryptoclidus* is a member, are famously typical marine reptiles, which lived in the Mesozoic era – 225–160 million years ago. Their shape is familiar, of course, from the many 'artists' impressions' and speculative reconstructions of Scotland's Loch Ness Monster. If 'Nessie' exists, it is likely that he or she is a plesiosaur. *Cryptoclidus* was no giant by some dinosaur standards; the specimen that used to be in the British Museum of Natural History was a mere 10ft (3m) long. These animals were well suited to a life under the ocean, having large flippers which moved up and down like a penguin's 'wings' or turtle's paddles, not back and forth like oars as their shape might suggest. It is thought that they would catch their diet of fish with darting movements of the long neck.

YOU WILL NEED
Scalpel or modelling knife
Scissors
Impact adhesive

2 sheets of minimum 16½ × 23⅜in (420 × 594mm) thick bright blue paper
1 sheet of minimum 16½ × 23⅜in (420 × 594mm) thick yellow paper
1 sheet of minimum 11¾ × 16½in (297 × 420mm) thin pink paper
1 sheet of minimum 8¼ × 11¾in (210 × 297mm) thick pink paper
Offcuts of white paper

1 Cut out the main body pieces and the two side body pieces from bright blue paper and cut the belly out from yellow paper.

2 Glue the main body pieces together, 1 to **1**.

3 Glue the body sides into place, 2 to **2**, and glue the ends 3 to **3**, and 4 to **4**.

4 Glue the belly into place 5 to **5**. Take care to align the limb holes.

5 Cut out two tail side pieces from blue paper and one tail base from yellow.

6 Glue the tail sides together, 6 to **6**.

7 Insert the tail base, 7 to **7**.

8 Glue the complete tail on to the body, 8 to **8.**

9 Cut out the seven pieces that make the neck from blue paper.

10 Glue 9 to **9** on piece 1 to form the first of many rings that fit together.

11 Glue 10 to **10** on piece 2. Glue piece 1 to piece 2, 11 to **11**.

12 Glue 12 to **12** on piece 3. Glue piece 2 to piece 3, 13 to **13**.

13 Glue 14 to **14** on piece 4. Glue piece 3 to piece 4, 15 to **15**.

14 Glue 16 to **16** on piece 5. Glue piece 4 to 5, 17 to **17**.

15 Glue 18 to **18** on piece 6. Glue piece 5 to 6, 19 to **19**.

16 Glue 20 to **20** on piece 7. Glue piece 6 to piece 7, 21 to **21**.

17 Cut out an upper and lower jaw from blue paper, but first stick the lower jaw to thin pink paper.

18 Cut out the palate from the thick pink paper.

19 On the upper jaw, glue 22 to **22** and 23 to **23**. Glue the palate into place in the upper jaw, 24 to **24**.

20 Glue 25 to **25** on the lower jaw. Stick the lower jaw to the upper jaw, 27 to **27**.

21 Cut out two eyes. Stick them to the head, 28 to **28**.

22 Cut out the teeth from white paper. Glue them into the mouth 29 to **29** in the lower, and to the palate, 30 to **30** in the upper.

23 Stick the head to the top of the neck, 31 to **31**, and the entire neck to the body, 32 to **32**.

24 Cut out two fins (stick the blue paper to pink first) and two arms from blue paper.

25 Glue 33 to **33** on the arm. Glue the fin to the arm, 34 to **34**.

26 Repeat this for the second fin, and then twice more with mirror image pieces for the two fins on the second side of the animal.

27 Glue the limbs to the body, 35 to **35**.

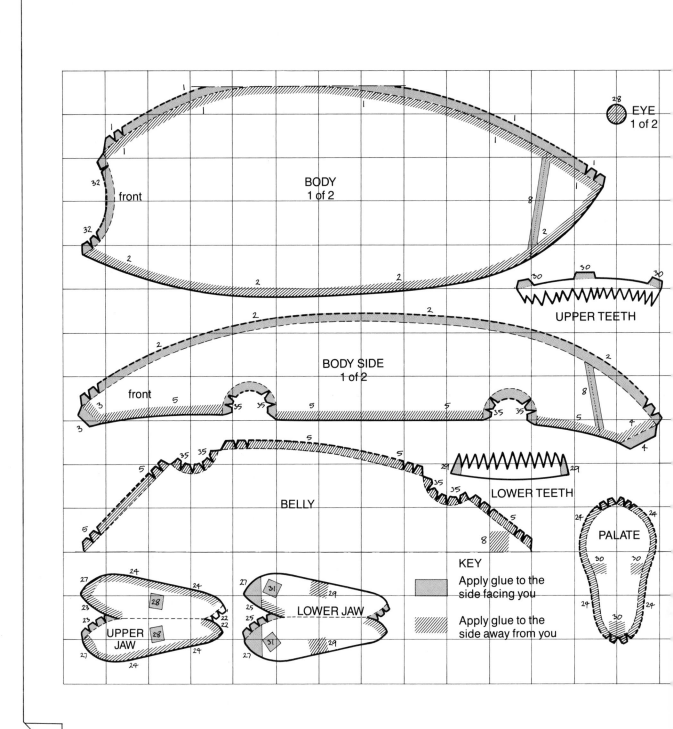

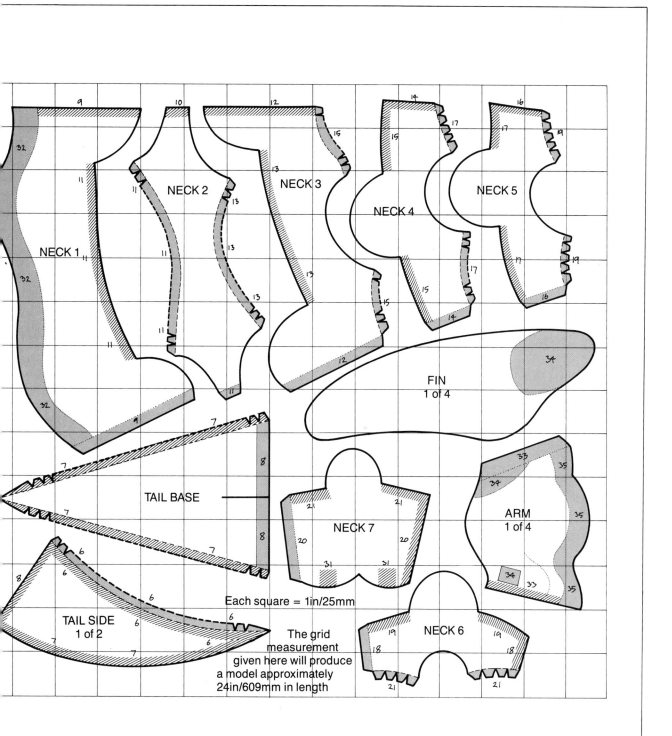

NECK 1

NECK 2

NECK 3

NECK 4

NECK 5

FIN
1 of 4

TAIL BASE

NECK 7

ARM
1 of 4

Each square = 1in/25mm

TAIL SIDE
1 of 2

The grid
measurement
given here will produce
a model approximately
24in/609mm in length

NECK 6

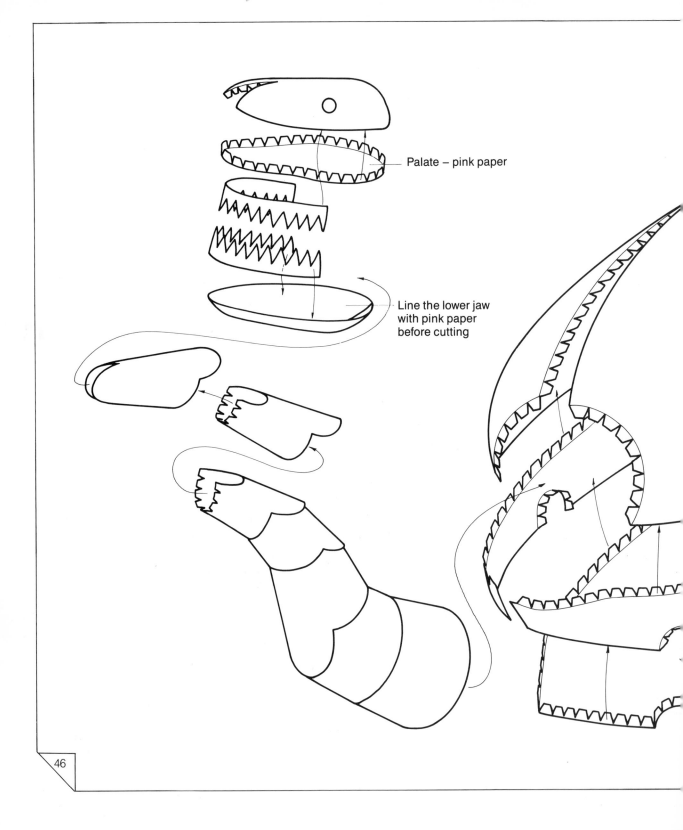

Palate – pink paper

Line the lower jaw
with pink paper
before cutting

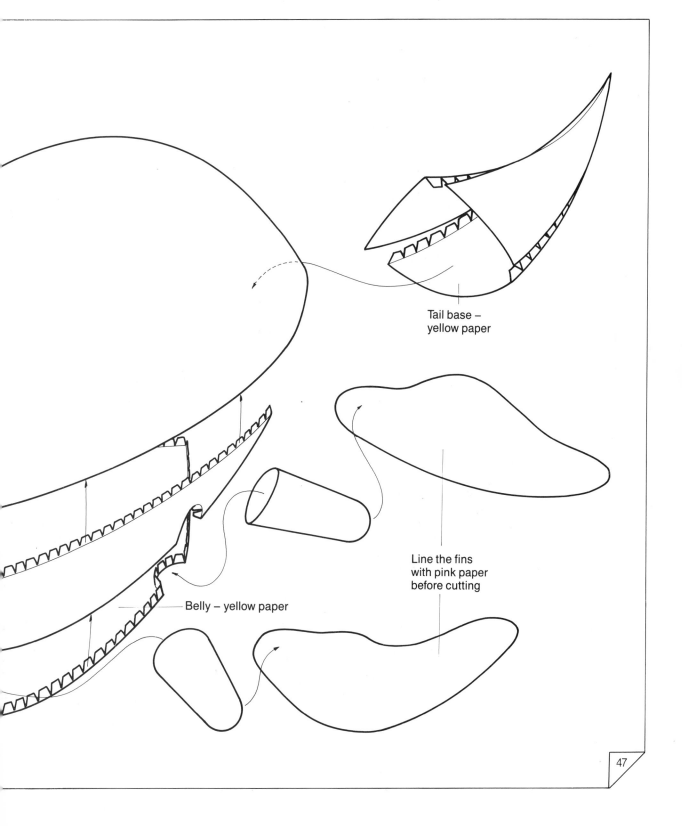

Tail base –
yellow paper

Line the fins
with pink paper
before cutting

Belly – yellow paper

ICHTHYOSAURUS ACUTIRUSTRIS

Looking and behaving far more like a fish than a reptile, Ichthyosaurs were the most highly marine-adapted dinosaur contemporaries, bearing some similarities to modern-day porpoises or dolphins. They have been traced as far back as the late Triassic era, but were most common in the Jurassic, extending somewhat into the early Cretaceous period (200–65 million years ago).

A number of very well-preserved skeletons of these animals, with their distinctive large eyes, have been found; some even retained the fossilized impressions of stomach contents, showing their diet – fish mainly, but the odd pterosaur for variety – and one with unborn young still in its belly. This revealed that Ichthyosaurs did not lay eggs like most reptiles, but bore their young alive, tail first, like porpoises. They were large, up to 30ft (9.4m), and fast; the flippers were apparently more steering aids than propulsive, the tail providing most of the motive power.

YOU WILL NEED
Scalpel or modelling knife
Scissors
Impact adhesive

2 sheets of minimum 16½×23⅜in (420×594mm) thick dark blue paper
1 sheet of minimum 16½×23⅜in (420×594mm) thick white paper
1 sheet of minimum 11¾×16½in (297×420mm) thin pink paper

1 Cut out two body sections from dark blue paper and the belly from white paper.

2 Glue the two dark blue body sections together, 1 to **1**.

3 Glue the belly into position 2 to **2**.

4 Glue 3 to **3** at the front of the body.

5 Cut out two eyes and colour as indicated in the photograph.

6 Fold and crease the eyes, then glue, 4 to **4**.

7 Glue the eye into the socket, 5 to **5**.

8 Insert the second eye in the same way.

9 Before cutting out the dark blue upper and lower beak, stick the blue paper to the thin pink paper, so that the inside of the model's open mouth will look more realistic.

10 Cut out the upper beak. Glue 6 to **6**.

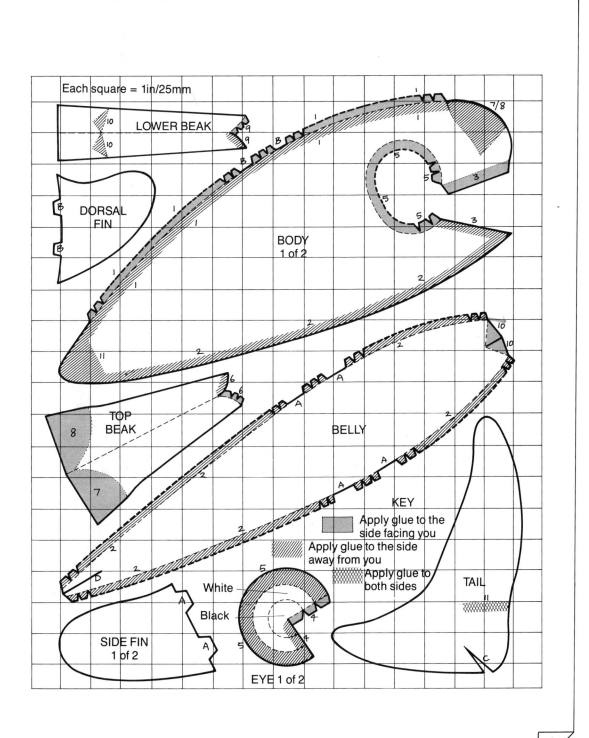

Each square = 1in/25mm

LOWER BEAK

DORSAL FIN

BODY 1 of 2

TOP BEAK

BELLY

KEY

Apply glue to the side facing you

Apply glue to the side away from you

Apply glue to both sides

TAIL

White

Black

SIDE FIN 1 of 2

EYE 1 of 2

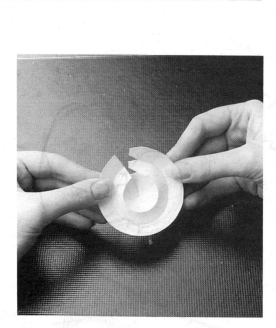

*The eye is folded and stuck to form
a cone shape.*

11 Glue the upper beak to the body, 7 to **7**
and 8 to **8**.

12 Cut out the lower beak and glue 9 to **9**.

13 Glue the lower beak to the body, 10 to **10**.

14 Before cutting out the side fins, stick the
dark blue paper to the white paper. Cut out
two side fins (one the mirror image of the
other).

15 Attach the fins to the body by matching
tabs A to slots **A**; ensure that the blue paper
faces upwards.

16 Cut out a dorsal fin from blue paper.
Attach it to the body by matching slots **B** in
the body to tabs B on the fin.

17 Cut out the tail from blue paper and stick
it to the body by interslotting slot C on the tail
and D on the body, then glue 11 to **11**.

CHICAGO HEIGHTS PUBLIC LIBRARY

j 745.592
H389 pap
.1

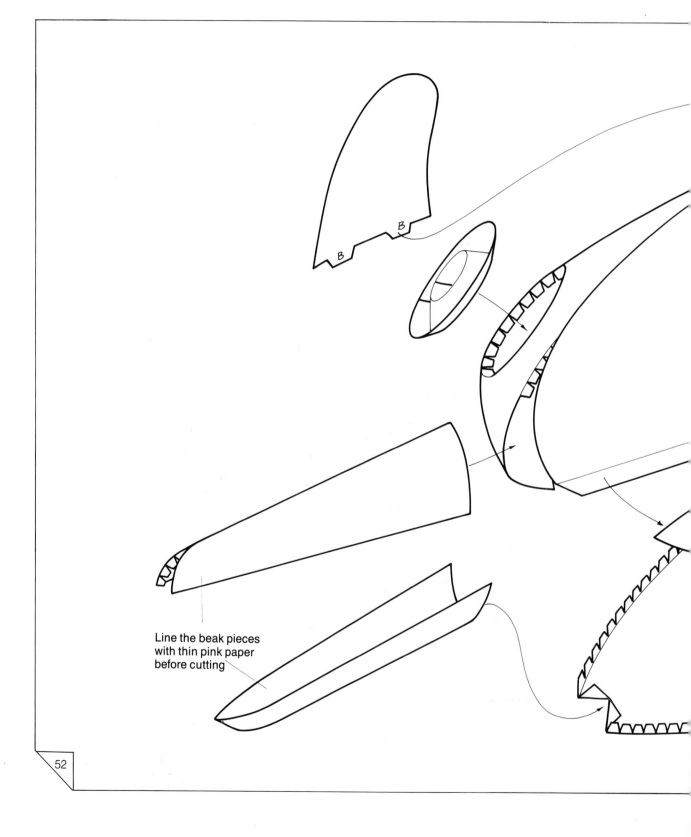

B

B

B

Line the beak pieces
with thin pink paper
before cutting

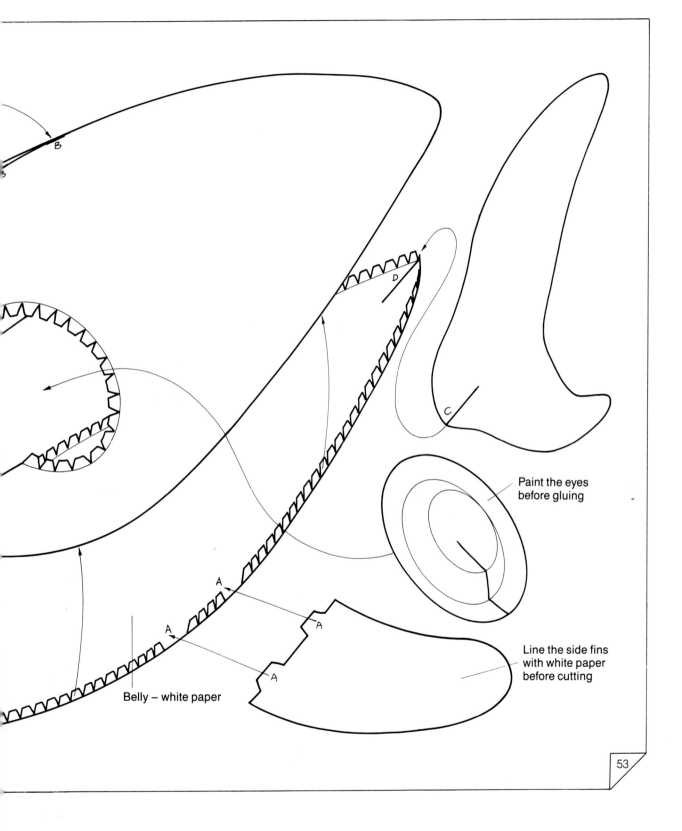

B

D

C

Paint the eyes
before gluing

A
A
A
A

Line the side fins
with white paper
before cutting

Belly – white paper

ARCHAEOPTERYX LITHOGRAPHICA

Is it a bird? Is it a reptile? The origins of *Archaeopteryx*, a fossilized skeleton of which was first discovered in south Germany in 1861, have been the subject of a celebrated dinosaur controversy ever since. The 'Lithographica' part of the name is the key; the skeleton was preserved in lithographic limestone, a particularly fine-grained stone used in printing for its capacity to retain detail. In this case the stone had preserved the impression not only of the bones, but of feathers around them. So began the argument, the latest development in which occurred in early 1988. Scientists, including Sir Fred Hoyle, denounced as fraudulent the feather impressions of the *Archaeopteryx* example in the British Museum of Natural History.

YOU WILL NEED
Scalpel or modelling knife
Scissors
Impact adhesive

2 sheets of minimum 17¾ × 25¼ in (450 × 640mm) thick bright blue paper
1 sheet of minimum 8¼ × 11¾ in (210 × 297mm) thick yellow paper
1 sheet of minimum 11¾ × 16½ in (297 × 420mm) thin yellow paper
1 sheet of minimum 8¼ × 11¾ in (210 × 297mm) thin pink paper
1 sheet of minimum 8¼ × 11¾ in (210 × 297mm) thick orange paper
Offcuts of red paper

1 Cut out the body from blue paper.

2 Cut out the breast details from thin yellow paper and stick these on to the body, 1 to **1**, 2 to **2**, 3 to **3** and 4 to **4**.

3 On the body, glue 5 to **5**, and 6 to **6**.

4 Glue 7 to **7**.

5 Cut out the five pieces that make the neck from blue paper. On piece 1 glue 8 to **8**.

6 On piece 2, glue 9 to **9**. Glue piece 1 to 2, 10 to **10**.

7 On piece 3, glue 11 to **11**. Glue piece 2 to piece 3, 12 to **12**.

8 On piece 4 glue 13 to **13**.

9 Glue piece 3 to 4, 14 to **14**.

10 On piece 5, glue 15 to **15**. Glue piece 4 to piece 5, 16 to **16**.

11 Glue the complete neck into the body, 17 to **17**.

12 Before cutting out the two halves of the head, stick a thin pink paper backing to the blue. Now cut them out and glue 18 to **18**, 19 to **19** on both halves.

13 Join the upper and lower head, 20 to **20**.

14 Cut out and glue the white teeth into place, 21 to **21**, 22 to **22** in both halves of the head.

15 Cut out two eyes from white paper and glue them into place, 23 to **23**.

16 Stick the head on to the end of the neck, 24 to **24**.

17 Cut out the tail from blue paper.

18 Glue it into place on the body, 25 to **25**. The slots tuck over so the outside edges of the tail come on top of the body.

19 Cut out the tail underside from thick yellow paper. Glue 26 to **26**. Then glue into the body, 27 to **27** and 28 to **28**.

20 Cut out the three pieces that make a wing, but first stick the wing tip onto thin yellow paper. The main wing is cut from blue paper, the feathers from orange paper.

21 Glue the wing tip to the main wing, 29 to **29**.

22 Glue 30 to **30** and 31 to **31** to finish the wing. Glue it into place on the body, 32 to **32** and 33 to **33**.

23 Repeat steps 20–22 for the second wing, using mirror image pieces.

24 Cut out a red tongue for the mouth, and add small red dots to the eyes.

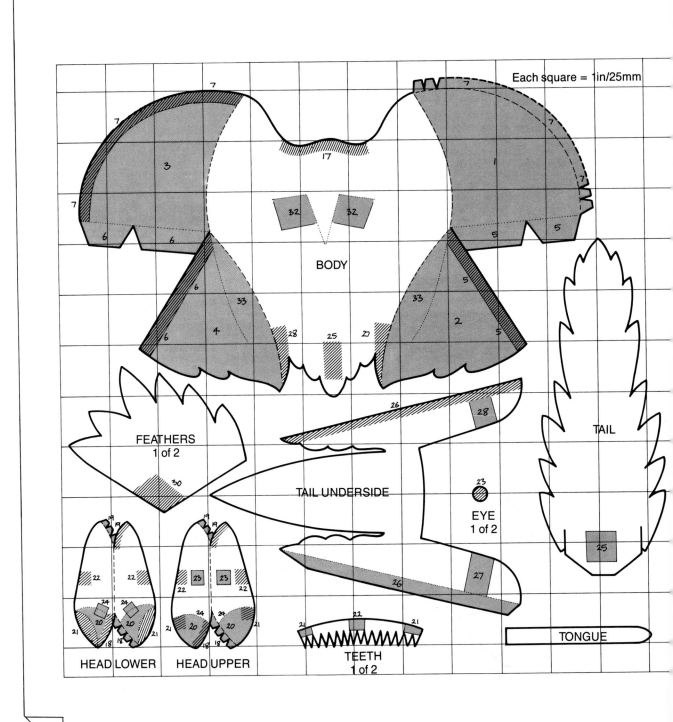

Each square = 1in/25mm

BODY

FEATHERS
1 of 2

TAIL UNDERSIDE

TAIL

EYE
1 of 2

HEAD LOWER   HEAD UPPER

TEETH
1 of 2

TONGUE

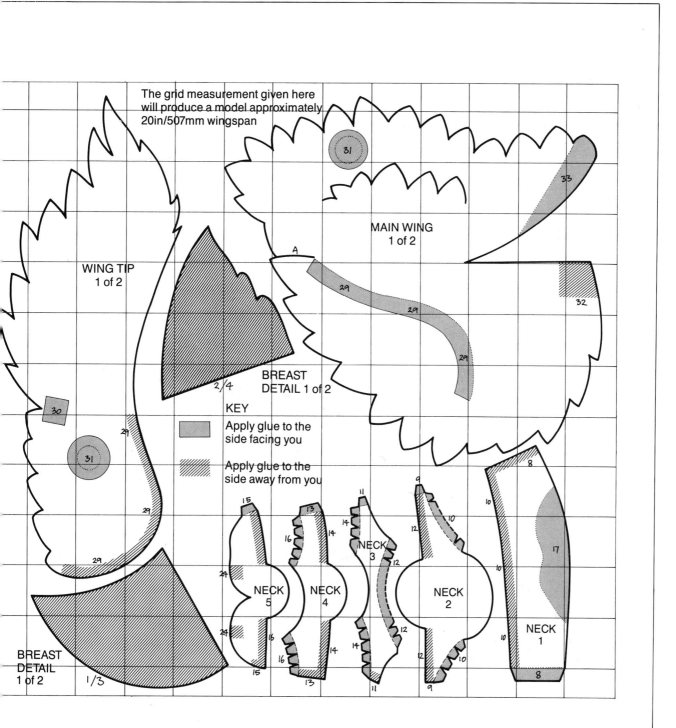

The grid measurement given here
will produce a model approximately
20in/507mm wingspan

31

33

MAIN WING
1 of 2

A

WING TIP
1 of 2

29

29

29

32

BREAST
DETAIL 1 of 2

30

KEY

2/4

Apply glue to the
side facing you

29

31

Apply glue to the
side away from you

8

9

17

29

15

11

10

13

29

16

14

14

10

NECK
3

10

12

12

NECK
2

NECK
5

NECK
4

10

189

24

NECK
1

24

16

14

14

12

10

BREAST
DETAIL
1 of 2

1/3

15

16

12

10

13

11

9

8

Tail underside – yellow paper

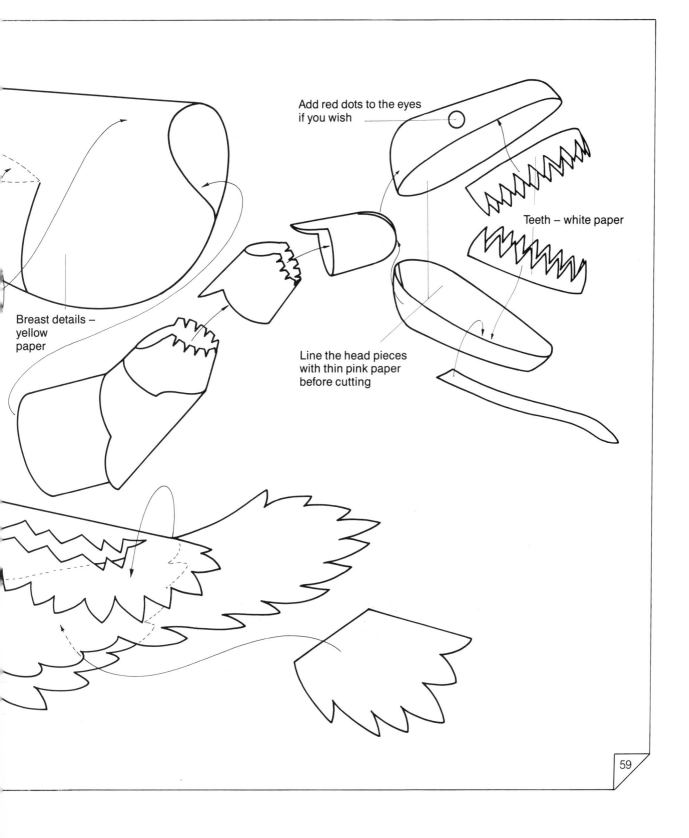

Add red dots to the eyes
if you wish

Teeth – white paper

Breast details –
yellow
paper

Line the head pieces
with thin pink paper
before cutting

PTERANODON

Pteranodon, a member of the Pterodactyloid family (Pterosaurs), was a highly developed creature with some very strange features, and thought to have been among the biggest of pterosaurs, with a wingspan of up to 23ft (7m) – until a find in Texas in 1972 of a pterosaur skeleton which indicated a 50ft (15m) wingspan, the size of a small aircraft!

Pteranodon, living in the late Jurassic period, 200 million years ago, had a long toothless beak which was counterbalanced by a long bony crest at the back of the head. It was an ocean-going fish eater – the Jurassic equivalent of the albatross – which helps to confirm the function of the crest in balancing the head as the animal dived into the waves for food. It also had a pouch of skin between the lower jaws where it could store food, much like modern pelicans. It is undoubtedly a reptile, and though the giant pterosaur from Texas has been named *Quetzalcoatlus* (feathered serpent, after an Aztec god), there is no evidence that either this monster or *Pteranodon* were actually feathered.

(See colour photograph at the foot of pages 66–67.)

YOU WILL NEED
Scalpel or modelling knife
Scissors
Impact adhesive

3 sheets of minimum 16½×23⅜in (420×594mm) thick pink paper
2 sheets of minimum 16½×23⅜in (420×594mm) thin lavender paper
1 sheet of minimum 11¾×16½in (297×420mm) thin pale pink paper
Offcuts of red paper

1 Cut out the body from thick pink paper. Cut out the lower body patterns from lavender paper and glue these on to the body, 1 to **1**, 2 to **2**, 3 to **3**, and 4 to **4**.

2 Glue 5 to **5** and 6 to **6** on the body.

3 Glue 7 to **7**.

4 Glue 8 to **8**, 9 to **9** and 10 to **10**.

5 Cut out the three pieces that make an arm. On the upper arm glue 11 to **11**.

6 On the lower arm glue 12 to **12**.

7 Join the upper and lower arm together, 13 to **13**.

8 Insert the elbow, 14 to **14**.

9 Cut out a hand from thick pink paper stuck to the thin pale pink paper.

10 Stick the hand to the end of the arm, 15 to **15**.

11 Cut out the three pieces that make the leg.

12 On the upper leg, glue 16 to **16**.

13 On the lower leg, glue 17 to **17**.

14 Join the upper and lower legs, 18 to **18**.

15 Insert the knee, 19 to **19**.

16 Cut out a foot from the thick pink paper stuck to thin pale pink paper.

17 Stick the foot into place on the end of the leg, 20 to **20**.

18 Repeat steps 5–17 with mirror image pieces for the remaining arm and leg.

19 Stick the legs into the body, 21 to **21**.

20 Cut out the five pieces that make the neck.

21 On piece 1 glue 22 to **22**.

22 On piece 2 glue 23 to **23**. Glue piece **1** to piece **2**, 24 to **24**.

23 Cut out piece **3**. Glue 25 to **25**. Glue piece **2** to piece **3**, 26 to **26**.

24 Cut out piece **4**. Glue 27 to **27**. Glue piece **3** to piece **4**, 28 to **28**.

25 Cut out piece **5**. Glue 29 to **29**. Glue piece **4** to piece **5**, 30 to **30**.

26 Glue the complete neck into the body, 31 to **31**.

27 Before cutting out a wing, stick the thick pink paper on to a lavender backing. Cut out a wing.

28 Stick the wing to the body, 32 to **32**, 33 to **33**, the lavender side facing down. The curve

created on the plane of the wing when gluing will keep it outstretched. Take the ready-constructed arm and glue it into the body and the wing, 34 to **34**, 35 to **35**.

29 Repeat this process with a mirror image wing and the second arm.

30 Cut out the four pieces that make the head, first sticking the thick pink paper to the thin pale pink paper.

31 Glue the two head sides together, 36 to **36**.

32 Glue 37 to **37** on the lower jaw, then stick the lower jaw to the head sides, 38 to **38** and 39 to **39**.

33 Fold up the upper jaw and glue 40 to **40**, then 41 to **41**.

34 Join the upper jaw and the lower jaw, 42 to **42** and 43 to **43**.

35 Cut out and colour two eyes as indicated in the photograph. Fold them up and glue 44 to **44**.

36 Stick them into the sockets on the head, 45 to **45**.

37 Cut out the two sides of the crest. Score them, fold them and glue 46 to **46** and 47 to **47**.

38 Stick the crest into the head, 48 to **48**, 49 to **49**, 50 to **50** and 51 to **51**.

39 Stick the complete head on to the neck, 52 to **52**.

40 Cut out the long, straight tongue from red paper and position it in the model's mouth as shown in the photograph.

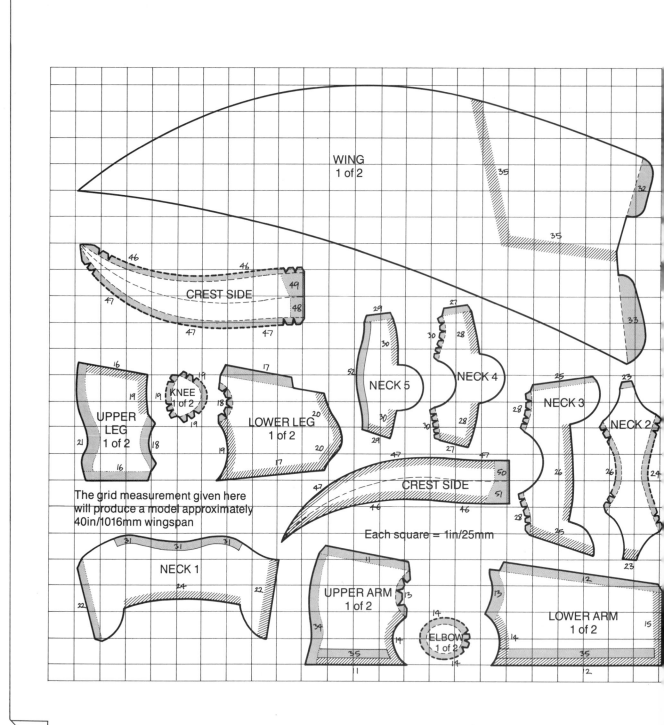

WING
1 of 2

35

32

35

33

CREST SIDE

46

46

47

49

48

47

47

UPPER
LEG
1 of 2

16

19

19

21

18

16

KNEE
1 of 2

17

17

19

19

LOWER LEG
1 of 2

17

18

20

19

17

20

NECK 5

29

30

52

30

29

30

NECK 4

27

30

28

28

27

NECK 3

25

28

25

NECK 2

23

26

26

24

28

23

The grid measurement given here
will produce a model approximately
40in/1016mm wingspan

CREST SIDE

47

47

50

47

46

46

51

Each square = 1in/25mm

NECK 1

31

31

31

24

22

22

UPPER ARM
1 of 2

11

13

34

14

1

35

ELBOW
1 of 2

14

14

LOWER ARM
1 of 2

12

13

15

14

35

2

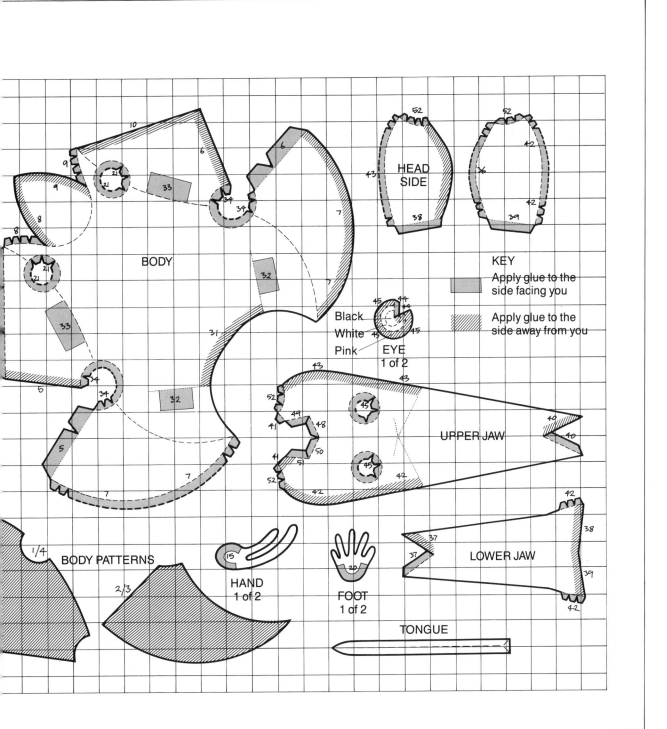

HEAD
SIDE

KEY

Apply glue to the
side facing you

Apply glue to the
side away from you

BODY

Black
White
Pink
EYE
1 of 2

UPPER JAW

LOWER JAW

BODY PATTERNS

1/4

2/3

HAND
1 of 2

FOOT
1 of 2

TONGUE

63

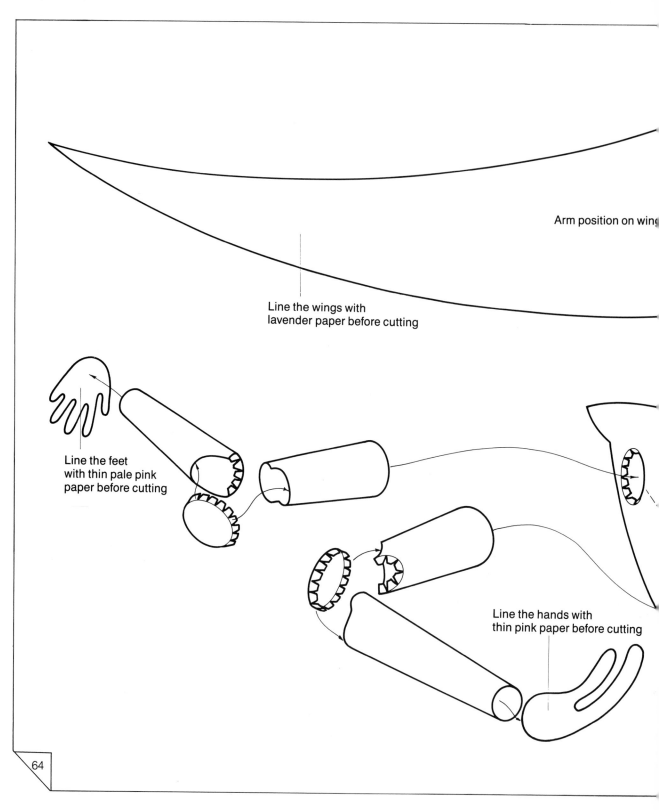

Arm position on wing

Line the wings with
lavender paper before cutting

Line the feet
with thin pale pink
paper before cutting

Line the hands with
thin pink paper before cutting

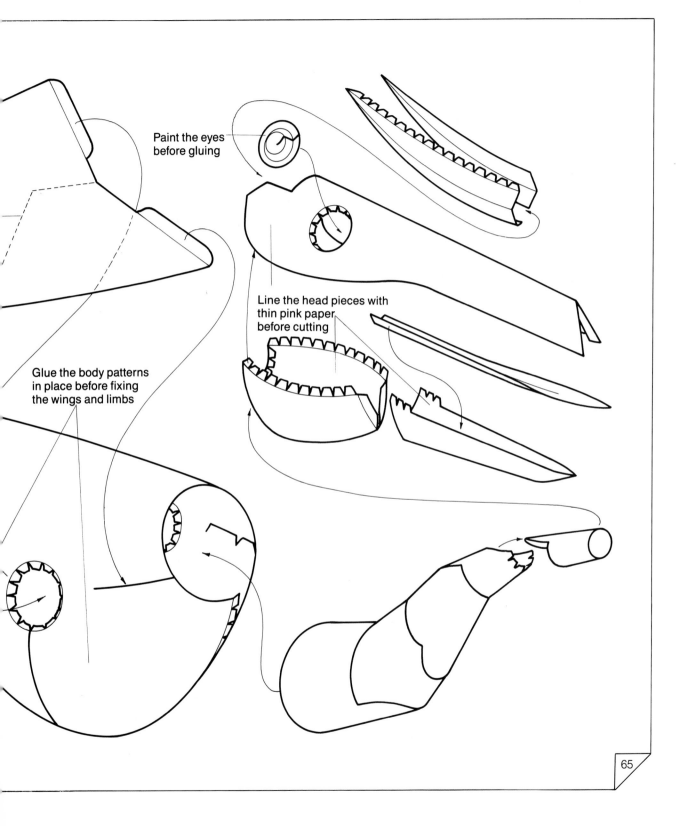

Paint the eyes before gluing

Line the head pieces with thin pink paper before cutting

Glue the body patterns in place before fixing the wings and limbs

65

Above: Eudimorphodon

Below: Pteranodon

EUDIMORPHODON

Eudimorphodon is a family member of the Pterosaurs, or wing reptiles, which lived at the same time as the dinosaurs, throughout the Triassic, Jurassic and Cretaceous periods. But they were creatures of the air, rather than the land. *Eudimorphodon* ('True two-form tooth') was of medium size (a 6ft (1.8m) wingspan), among a range of Pterodactyls that went from sparrow size to giants with 50ft (15.24m) wingspans. Most Pterosaur remains have been found in marine deposits, which suggest that they were marine-based creatures themselves. The arrangement of the rows of sharp, densely packed teeth also indicate a diet of fish. But their bones were light – many with cavities, to assist flight – and fossilization would have been far less possible for the inland versions.

(See colour photograph at the top of page 66.)

YOU WILL NEED
Scalpel or modelling knife
Scissors
Impact adhesive

1 sheet of minimum 8¼ × 11¾ in (210 × 297mm) thick white paper
3 sheets of minimum 17¾ × 25¼ in (450 × 640mm) thick rose pink paper
1 sheet of minimum 17¾ × 25¼ in (450 × 640mm) thin yellow paper
1 sheet of minimum 8¼ × 11¾ in (210 × 297mm) thick pale pink paper
1 sheet of minimum 8¼ × 11¾ in (210 × 297mm) thin pink paper
Offcuts of red paper

1 Cut out the body from rose pink paper and the belly patterns from yellow. Stick the four pieces of pattern on to the body before any folding is done, 1 to **1**, 2 to **2**, 3 to **3**, 4 to **4**.

2 On the body, glue 5 to **5** and 6 to **6**.

3 Glue 7 to **7**.

4 Glue 8 to **8**, 9 to **9** and 10 to **10** for the tail.

5 Cut out the three pieces that form the neck. On piece one, glue 11 to **11**.

6 On piece two, glue 12 to **12**. Glue piece one to piece two, 13 to **13**.

7 On piece three, glue 14 to **14**. Glue piece two to piece three, 15 to **15**.

8 Cut out the upper jaw from rose pink paper and cut the palate from thick pale pink paper.

9 On the upper jaw glue 16 to **16** and 17 to **17**.

10 Insert the palate 18 to **18**.

11 Before cutting out the lower jaw, first stick the rose pink paper to a thin piece of pink backing paper.

12 On the lower jaw, glue 19 to **19** and 20 to **20**.

13 Cut out two eyes and colour them as indicated. Fold up and glue 21 to **21**.

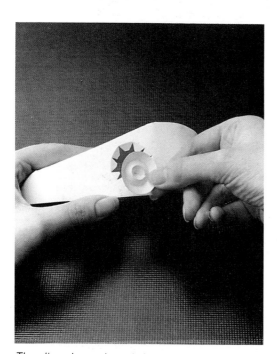

The disc-shaped eye is lowered into position in the head.

14 Stick the eyes into position in the eye sockets in the head, 22 to **22**.

15 Stick the lower and upper jaws together, 23 to **23**.

16 Glue the white paper teeth into position, 24 to **24**.

17 Cut out the three pieces that make the arm from rose pink paper.

18 Glue 25 to **25** on the upper arm.

19 Glue 26 to **26** on the lower arm.

20 Join the upper and lower arm, 27 to **27**.

21 Insert the elbow 28 to **28**.

22 Stick the complete arm into the body, 29 to **29**.

23 Repeat stages 18–22 for the second arm.

24 Cut out the three pieces that make the leg from rose pink paper. Also cut out the foot from rose pink paper.

25 Glue 30 to **30** on the upper leg.

26 Glue 31 to **31** on the lower leg.

27 Join the upper and lower legs, 32 to **32**.

28 Insert the knee, 33 to **33**.

29 Stick the leg into the body, 34 to **34**.

30 Fold and glue the foot together, 35 to **35**, 36 to **36**, 37 to **37**, 38 to **38**, 39 to **39**, and 40 to **40**.

31 Glue the complete foot into place on the end of the leg, 41 to **41** and 42 to **42**.

32 Repeat instructions for the second leg.

33 Cut out the wings, one a mirror image of the other.

34 Glue 43 to **43**.

35 Stick the wing on to the arm/body assembly, 44 to **44**, 45 to **45**, 46 to **46**.

36 Finish the model by repeating steps 35 and 36 with the mirror image wing, cutting out and gluing the red tongue as you wish, and cutting out the white claws for the wings and feet.

37 Glue the claws to the wings, 47 to **47**: glue the claws together for the feet, 48 to **48**, then glue them to the feet, 49 to **49**.

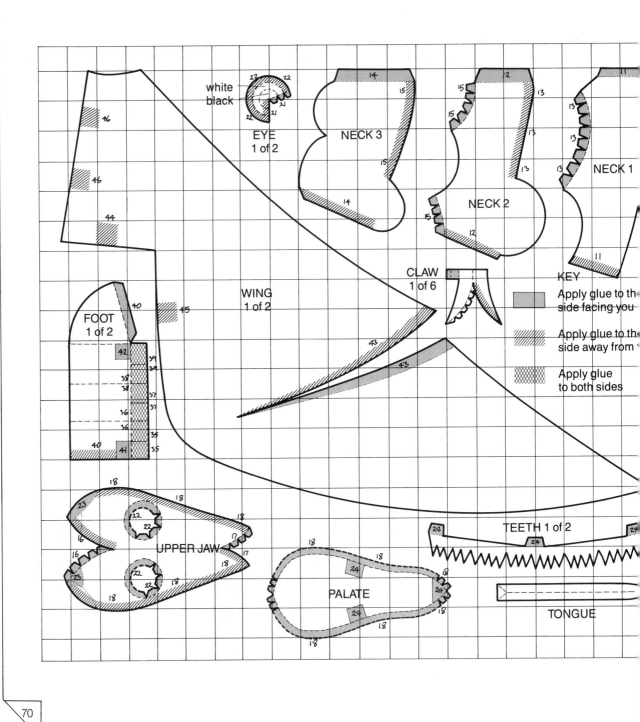

white
black

EYE
1 of 2

NECK 3

NECK 1

NECK 2

CLAW
1 of 6

WING
1 of 2

KEY

Apply glue to the
side facing you

Apply glue to the
side away from

Apply glue
to both sides

FOOT
1 of 2

UPPER JAW

PALATE

TEETH 1 of 2

TONGUE

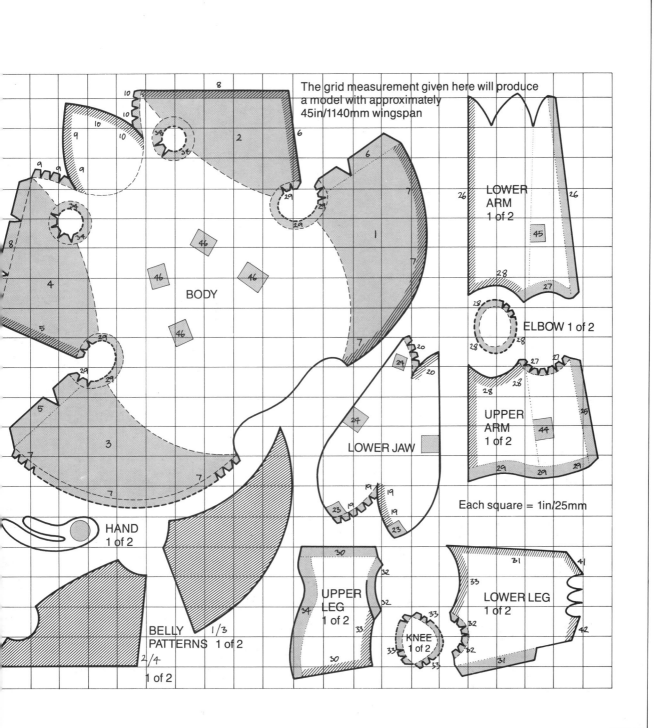

The grid measurement given here will produce a model with approximately 45in/1140mm wingspan

BODY

LOWER ARM 1 of 2

ELBOW 1 of 2

UPPER ARM 1 of 2

Each square = 1in/25mm

LOWER JAW

HAND 1 of 2

BELLY PATTERNS 1 of 2

UPPER LEG 1 of 2

KNEE 1 of 2

LOWER LEG 1 of 2

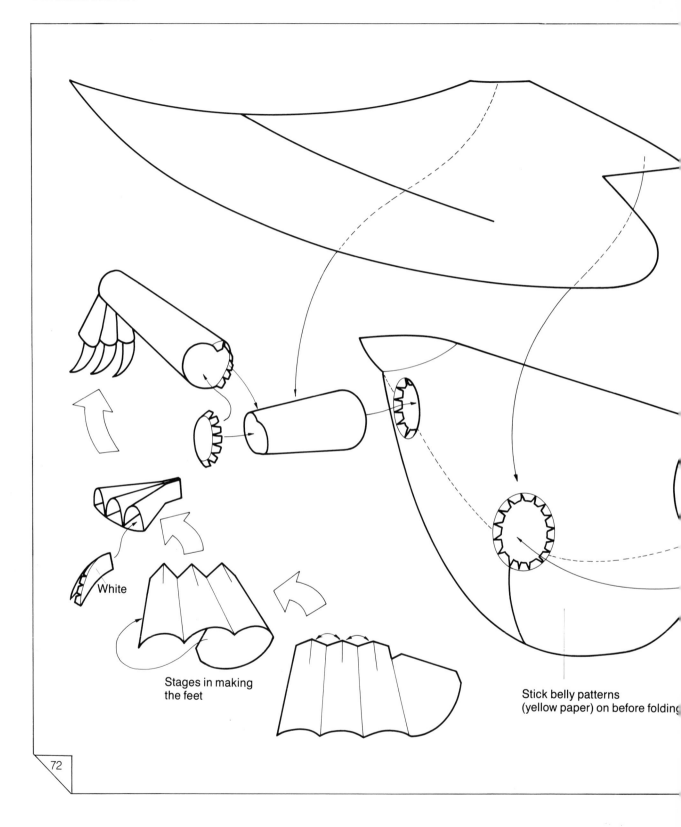

White

Stages in making
the feet

Stick belly patterns
(yellow paper) on before folding

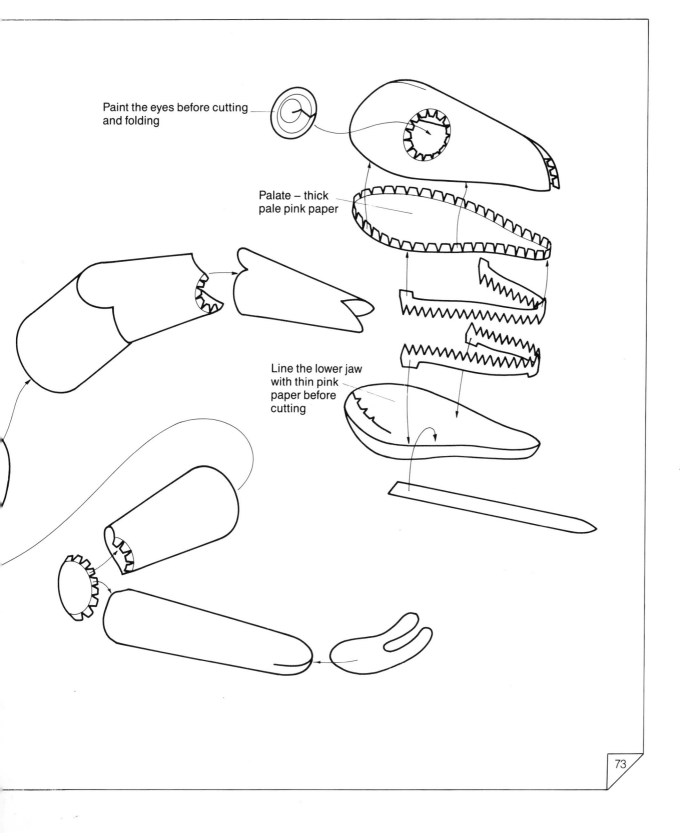

Paint the eyes before cutting and folding

Palate – thick pale pink paper

Line the lower jaw with thin pink paper before cutting

OURANOSAURUS

Ouranosaurus is a comparatively recent find. A well-preserved skeleton was discovered in Nigeria, West Africa, in 1965. It was a member of the Iguanadontid family which were distinguished by their size (up to 33ft (10m) long), their short but strong front limbs and their enormously powerful legs. It lived in the mid-Cretaceous period, 110–100 million years ago, and was likely to have lived in herds – it was a vegetarian, and thus vulnerable to predators; and fed on the kind of herbiage that grows in marshy areas.

Ouranosaurus, however, is distinguished by its extraordinary sail-like spine, a covering of skin stretched over hugely extended bones of the vertebrae. The elongated sections are more than twice as high as those of *Iguanadon*. *Stegosaurus* and *Dimetrodon*, of course, also displayed this unusual characteristic; it is thought to have acted as a 'heat exchanger', helping to absorb warmth from the sun in the early morning after a cold desert night, and dissipate it during the hot days.

(See colour photograph at the top of page 78.)

YOU WILL NEED
Scalpel or modelling knife
Scissors
Impact adhesive

3 sheets of minimum 16½ × 23⅜in (420×594mm) thick orange paper
1 sheet of minimum 16½ × 23⅜in (420×594mm) thick yellow paper
1 sheet of minimum 8¼ × 11¾in (210×297mm) thick white paper
1 sheet of minimum 16½ × 23⅜in (420×594mm) thin pink paper
Offcuts of red paper

1 Cut out the two sides of the body from orange paper, and the belly from yellow.

2 On the body, glue 1 to **1**.

3 Glue the two sides of the body together, 2 to **2**.

4 Insert the belly and glue 3 to **3**.

5 Cut out the three pieces that make a leg from orange paper, and then cut out a foot, also from orange paper.

6 On the upper leg glue 4 to **4**.

7 On the lower leg glue 5 to **5**.

8 Join the upper and lower legs, 6 to **6**.

9 Insert the knee, 7 to **7**.

10 Fold up and glue the foot, 8 to **8**.

11 Glue the foot to the base of the leg, 9 to **9**, and stick the white 'toenails' on.

12 Stick the leg into the body, 10 to **10**.

13 Repeat steps 5–12 using mirror image pieces for the second leg.

14 Cut out the two pieces that make the arm and a hand.

15 On the upper arm glue 11 to **11**.

16 On the lower arm glue 12 to **12**.

17 Join the upper and lower arms, 13 to **13**.

18 On the lower arm glue 14 to **14**.

19 On the hand glue 15 to **15** and 16 to **16**.

20 Glue 17 to **17**, 18 to **18**, 19 to **19** and 20 to **20**.

21 Glue the hand into place 21 to **21** and 22 to **22**. Cut out, fold and glue the claws and 'thumb' to the hand and arm.

22 Glue the arm into place in the body, 23 to **23**.

23 Repeat steps 14–22 for the second arm. Use mirror image pieces.

24 Cut out the four pieces that form the neck from orange paper.

25 On piece 1 glue 24 to **24**.

26 On piece 2 glue 25 to **25**: join piece 1 to piece 2, 26 to **26**.

27 On piece 3 glue 27 to **27**.

28 Glue piece 2 to piece 3, 28 to **28**.

29 On piece 4, glue 29 to **29**. Glue piece 3 to 4, 30 to **30**.

30 Glue the neck to the body, 31 to **31**.

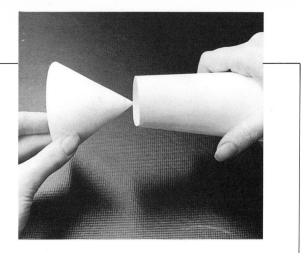

The foot (a simple cone shape) is stuck in place at the end of the leg.

31 Cut out the four pieces that form the head, but first glue the orange paper to the thin pink paper.

32 On the head top, glue 32 to **32**.

33 Glue the head side into place, 34 to **34**, 33 to **33** and 35 to **35**.

34 Repeat for the second side, 36 to **36**, 37 to **37**, 38 to **38**.

35 Glue the lower jaw together, 39 to **39**, then glue it in position on the head sides, 40 to **40**, and 41 to **41**. Cut out and glue in the teeth.

36 Cut out two small eyes and stick them into position on the head, 42 to **42**. Draw a dot in the centre of each.

37 Glue the complete head on to the neck, 43 to **43**.

38 Make the tail exactly the same as for the *Tyrannosaurus Rex* (see page 8), and stick it on to the body.

39 Cut out the crest, cut out and stick the yellow decoration into place and slot the crest into the body and tail.

40 Cut out the tongue from red paper and position it in the model's mouth.

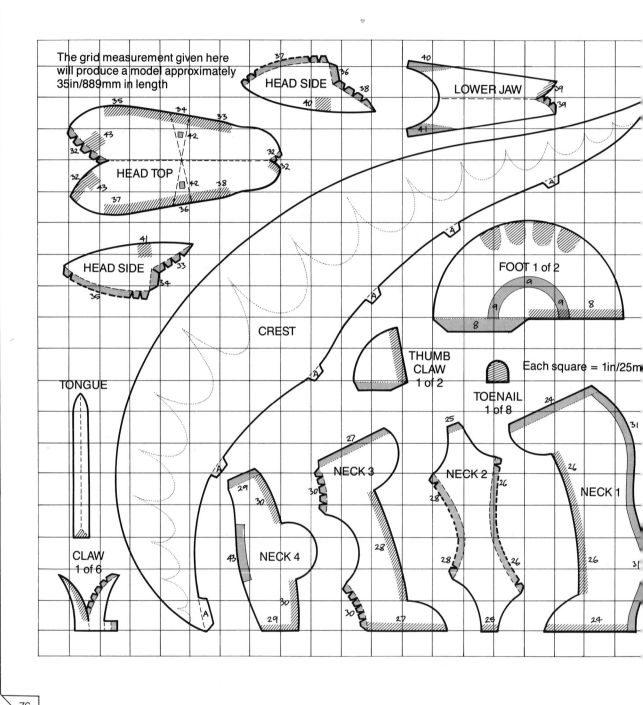

The grid measurement given here will produce a model approximately 35in/889mm in length

HEAD SIDE

LOWER JAW

HEAD TOP

HEAD SIDE

FOOT 1 of 2

CREST

THUMB CLAW 1 of 2

TOENAIL 1 of 8

Each square = 1in/25m

TONGUE

NECK 3

NECK 2

NECK 1

CLAW 1 of 6

NECK 4

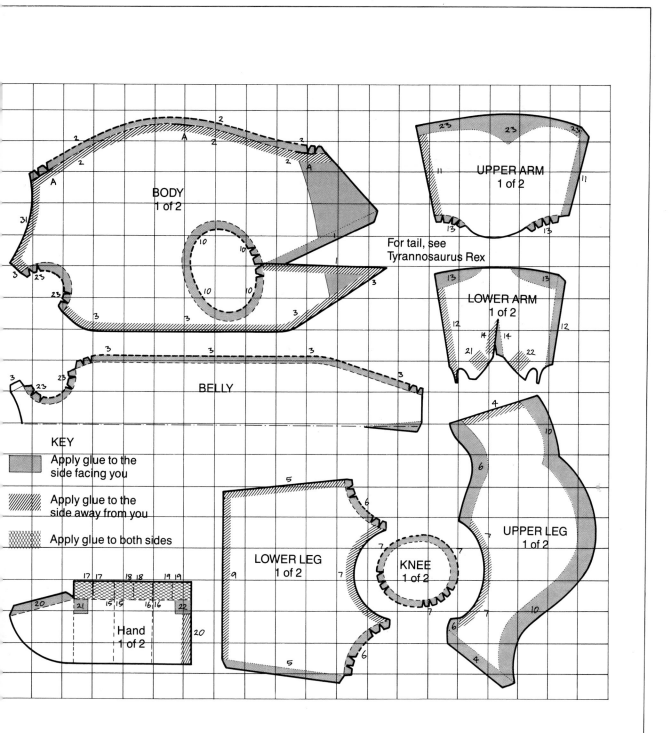

KEY

Apply glue to the side facing you

Apply glue to the side away from you

Apply glue to both sides

BODY
1 of 2

BELLY

For tail, see
Tyrannosaurus Rex

UPPER ARM
1 of 2

LOWER ARM
1 of 2

UPPER LEG
1 of 2

LOWER LEG
1 of 2

KNEE
1 of 2

Hand
1 of 2

Above: Ouranosaurus

Below: Euoplocephalus

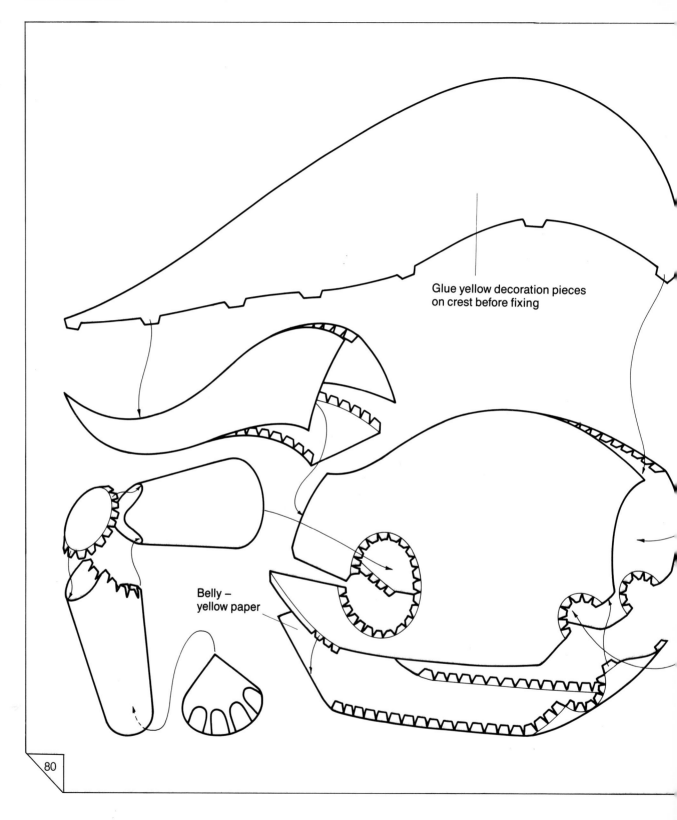

Glue yellow decoration pieces
on crest before fixing

Belly –
yellow paper

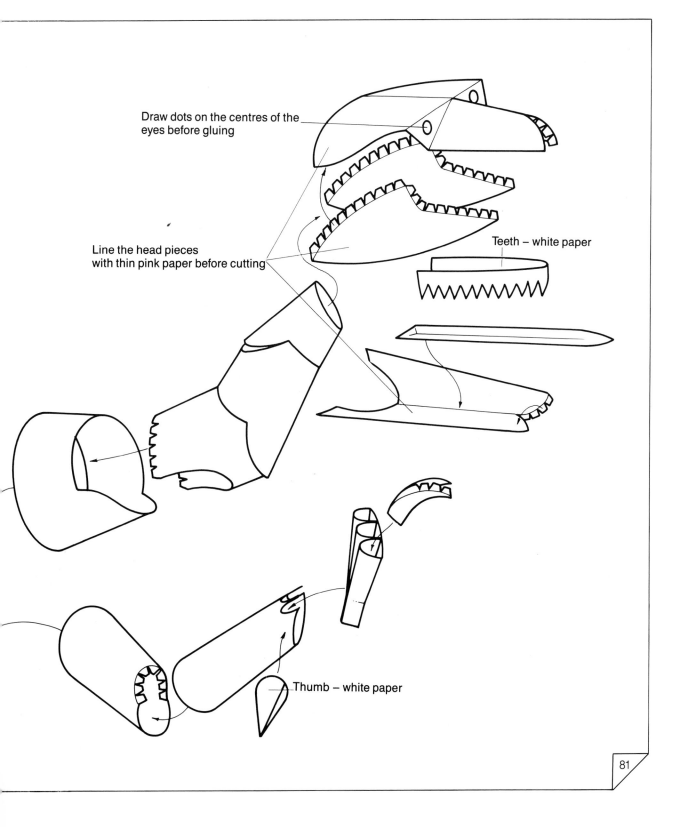

Draw dots on the centres of the
eyes before gluing

Line the head pieces
with thin pink paper before cutting

Teeth – white paper

Thumb – white paper

EUOPLOCEPHALUS

Euoplocephalus was a member of the Ankylosaur family (literally 'fused joined-together reptile'), all of which were distinguished by their heavily armour-plated skins. Bones in the skin, arranged in bands to allow reasonable flexibility, covered almost the entire animal's back; the head was covered with large slabs of bone, extending to the jaws and even in some cases the eyelids! The backbones made ridges of bony 'horns', which were also found round the neck and head. The final and most bizarre characteristic of all was the 'tail-club', which could be swung with great force – the tail muscles were huge – and acted primarily as a defence mechanism. It could also, it is assumed, be used in attack.

(See colour photograph at the foot of pages 78–79.)

YOU WILL NEED
Scalpel or modelling knife
Scissors
Impact adhesive

3 sheets of minimum 16½ × 23⅜in (420 × 594mm) thick grey paper
1 sheet of minimum 16½ × 23⅜in (420 × 594mm) thick pink paper
1 sheet of minimum 11¾ × 16½in (297 × 420mm) thin pink paper
1 sheet of minimum 16½ × 23⅜in (420 × 594mm) silver foil
Offcuts of red and white paper

1 Cut out body pieces 1, 2, 3, 5, 6 from grey paper.

2 Cut out body piece 4 from thick pink paper.

3 Glue piece 1 to 2 (5), 1 to **1**.

4 Glue pieces 1 and 2 (5) to 3 and 6, 2 to **2**.

5 Glue pieces 1, 2 (5) and 3 (6) to 4, 3 to **3**.

6 Glue 4 to **4** on top of body, 1.

7 Cut out two tail 'tops' from grey paper. Cut out two tail bottoms from thick pink paper.

8 Glue the two tops together, 5 to **5**.

9 Glue the two bottoms together, 6 to **6**.

10 Glue the top to the bottom, 7 to **7**.

11 Cut out the two pieces that form the tail club from grey paper. Note that one of them has no tabs.

12 Glue 8 to **8**, forming a cone.

13 Glue the two sides to each other, 9 to **9**, taking care to align the tail hole.

14 Slip the club on to the tip of the tail, 10 to **10**.

15 Glue the completed tail to the body, 11 to **11**. The tail will curve upwards.

16 Cut out the three pieces that form the front leg from grey paper.

17 Glue 12 to **12** on the upper leg.

18 Glue 13 to **13** on the lower leg.

19 Glue the upper to the lower leg, 14 to **14**.

20 Insert the knee, 15 to **15**.

21 Cut out the three pieces that form the back leg from grey paper.

22 Glue 16 to **16** on the upper leg.

23 Glue 17 to **17** on the lower leg.

24 Join the upper and lower leg together, 18 to **18**.

25 Insert the knee, 19 to **19**.

26 Join the front leg to the body, 20 to **20**.

27 Join the back leg to the body, 21 to **21**.

28 Repeat steps 16–27 with mirror image pieces for the other two legs.

29 Cut out the neck from grey paper. Glue 22 to **22**.

30 Join the neck to the body, 23 to **23**.

31 Before cutting out the four pieces that make up the head, stick them to some thin pale pink paper.

32 Cut out the four pieces that make the head from grey paper.

33 On the upper jaw, glue 24 to **24**.

34 Glue the upper jaw to the snout, 25 to **25**.

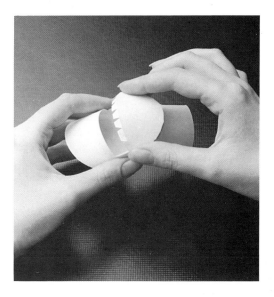

The kneecap is inserted between the upper and lower legs.

35 Glue 26 to **26** on the lower jaw.

36 Glue 27 to **27** on the lower jaw.

37 Join the upper and lower jaws with the 'jowl', 28 to **28**, 29 to **29**.

38 Colour the eyes as indicated to enhance the model's final appearance.

39 Fold up the eyes and glue 30 to **30**.

40 Insert the eyes into the head, 31 to **31**.

41 Cut out several silver or white 'toenails' and stick them at the end of each leg, 32 to **32**.

42 Cut out the silver 'armour plating' details, horns etc, and arrange them over the body.

43 Cut out the tongue from red paper and position it in the model's mouth.

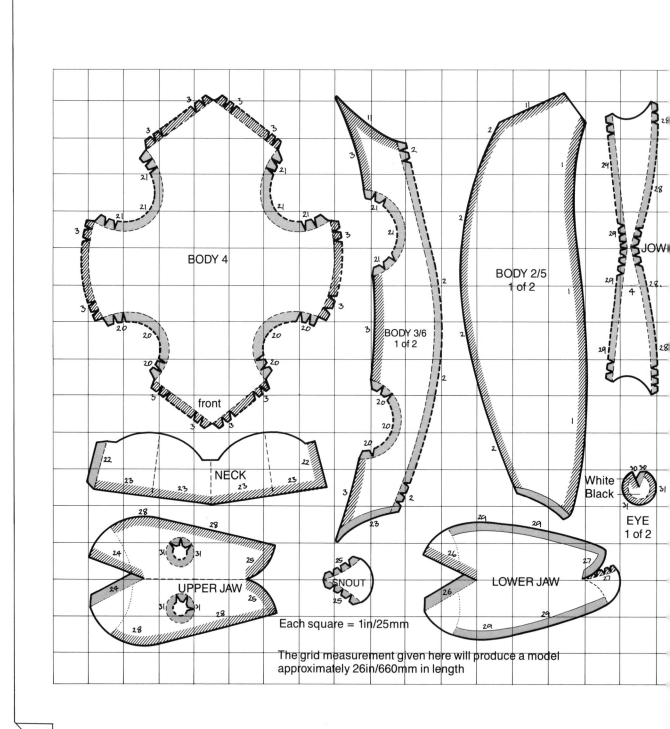

BODY 4

front

NECK

BODY 3/6
1 of 2

BODY 2/5
1 of 2

JOW

White
Black

EYE
1 of 2

UPPER JAW

SNOUT

LOWER JAW

Each square = 1in/25mm

The grid measurement given here will produce a model
approximately 26in/660mm in length

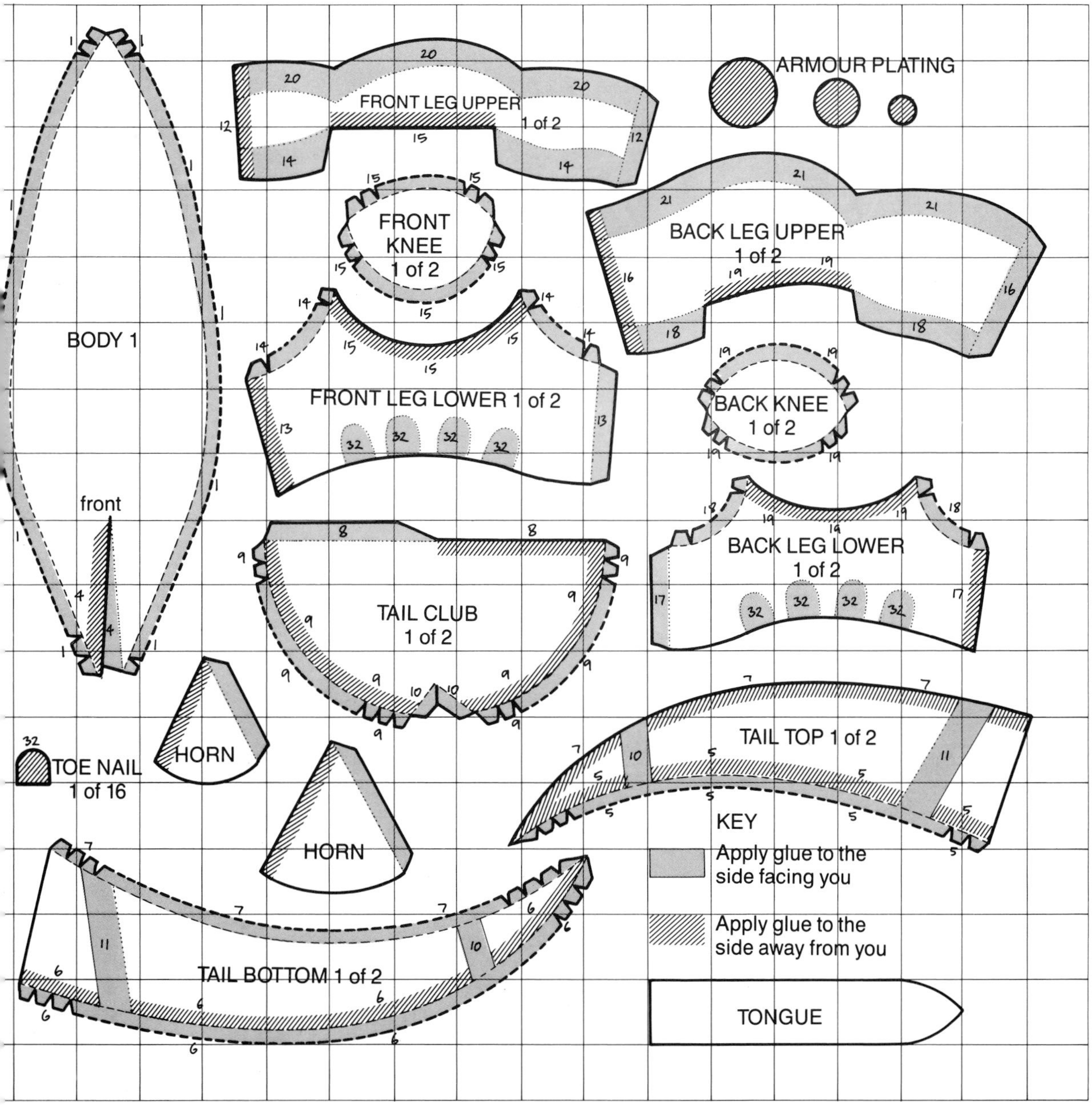

BODY 1

front

FRONT LEG UPPER
1 of 2

ARMOUR PLATING

FRONT
KNEE
1 of 2

BACK LEG UPPER
1 of 2

FRONT LEG LOWER 1 of 2

BACK KNEE
1 of 2

TAIL CLUB
1 of 2

BACK LEG LOWER
1 of 2

TOE NAIL
1 of 16

HORN

HORN

TAIL TOP 1 of 2

KEY

Apply glue to the
side facing you

Apply glue to the
side away from you

TAIL BOTTOM 1 of 2

TONGUE

Paint the eyes before
cutting and
folding

Line all four head pieces with
pale pink paper before cutting

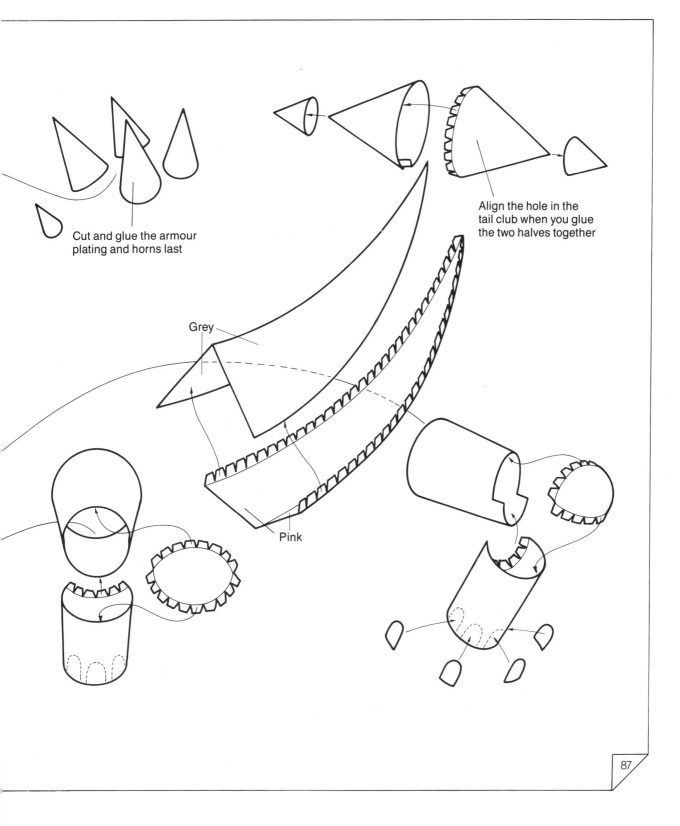

Cut and glue the armour
plating and horns last

Align the hole in the
tail club when you glue
the two halves together

Grey

Pink

EUSTHENOPTERON

These fish are very significant in the history of life on earth because, it is believed, the first land-living vertebrates (amphibians) evolved from them.

The name, meaning 'lobe fin', derives from the scaly, muscular stubby 'limbs' that carry the fins. It is from these that the arms and legs of land-living animals are thought to have developed. *Eusthenopteron* lived in Devonian times, 395 million years ago, and so came far earlier in the scheme of things than most of the dinosaurs in this book. They grew to about 2ft (60cm) in length, and were carnivorous; they would have used their lobes to support their weight in shallow water, and perhaps they were also capable of moving very sluggishly on land. A significant evolutionary characteristic is that they possessed lungs, and so could gulp at air. Land dwelling, however, would only have been in cases of dire necessity for *Eusthenopteron* – if the water of its natural habitat dried up, for instance.

A few examples of this kind of fish live today, notably the Australian lungfish and the coelocanth, thought to have been extinct for 65 million years until one was caught quite recently.

(See colour photograph at the top of page 95.)

YOU WILL NEED
Scalpel or modelling knife
Scissors
Impact adhesive

2 sheets of minimum 16½×23⅜in (420×594mm) gold card
1 sheet of minimum 16½×23⅜in (420×594mm) thick pale grey paper
1 sheet of minimum 11¾×16½in (297×420mm) thin pale pink paper

1 Cut two upper body pieces from gold card.

2 Cut two lower body sections from the pale grey paper.

3 Glue the two upper body pieces together, 1 to **1**.

4 Glue the two lower body sections together, 2 to **2**.

5 Join the upper and lower bodies, 3 to **3**.

6 Before cutting the lower jaw from pale grey paper, line it with thin pink paper.

7 Cut out the lower jaw and glue it, 4 to **4**.

8 Stick the lower jaw into position on the body, 5 to **5**.

9 Cut out the forehead from gold card. Stick it into position 6 to **6**.

10 Cut out the eyes and colour them as indicated in the photograph on page 95.

11 Fold them up and glue them 7 to **7**.

12 Stick the eyes into the eye sockets, 8 to **8**.

13 Cut out a large gill from gold card. Stick it into position, 9 to **9**.

14 Cut out a smaller gill from the gold card. Push tab A into slot **A**.

15 Repeat steps 13 and 14 for the opposite side of the fish.

16 Stick pink paper on to the gold card to line it, then cut out the six fins all together.

17 Cut out three 'arms' and glue 10 to **10** in each case.

18 Glue a fin on to the arm 11 to **11**.

19 Glue the fin/arm to the body, 12 to **12**.

20 Repeat this process for each fin, using mirror image pieces for the three remaining fins. Ensure that the gold side faces upwards.

21 Cut out a large and small dorsal fin from two pieces of gold paper stuck back to back so that it is gold on *both* sides.

22 Insert the large dorsal fin into the body, tab B to slot **B**.

23 Insert the small dorsal fin into the body, tab C to slot **C**.

24 Cut out the tail from two pieces of gold card stuck back to back. Again, this will show gold both sides.

25 Slide the tail into position at the back of the fish, gluing 13 to **13**.

The fin is glued to the end of the arm.

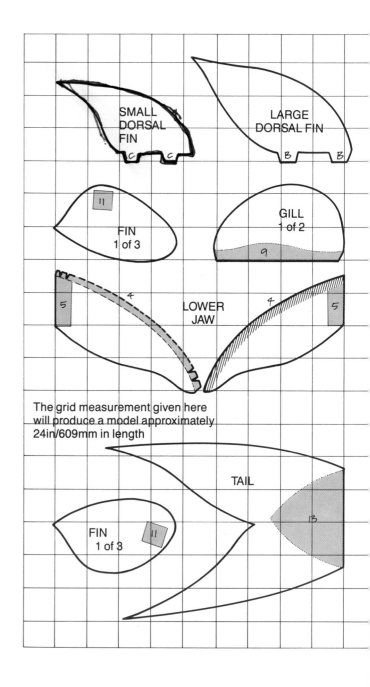

SMALL DORSAL FIN

LARGE DORSAL FIN

FIN
1 of 3

GILL
1 of 2

LOWER
JAW

The grid measurement given here
will produce a model approximately
24in/609mm in length

FIN
1 of 3

TAIL

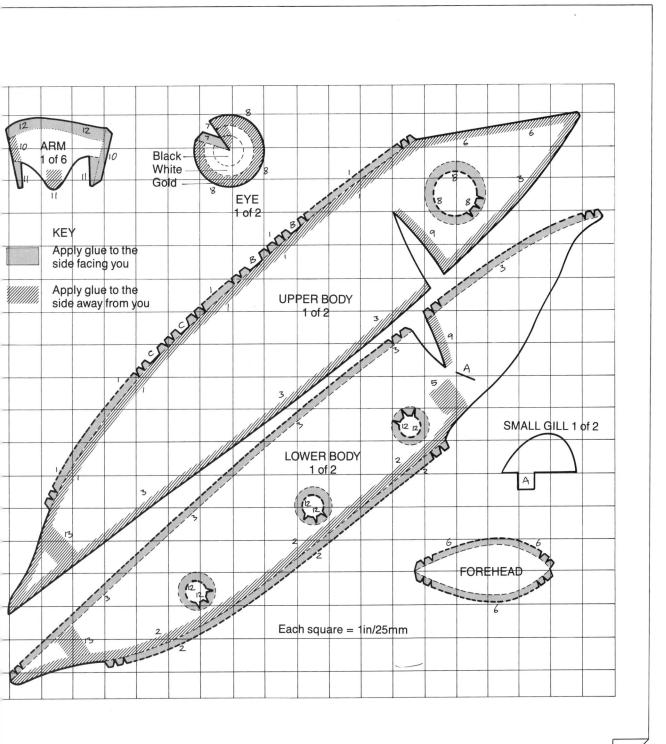

ARM
1 of 6

EYE
1 of 2

Black
White
Gold

KEY

Apply glue to the
side facing you

Apply glue to the
side away from you

UPPER BODY
1 of 2

LOWER BODY
1 of 2

SMALL GILL 1 of 2

A

FOREHEAD

Each square = 1in/25mm

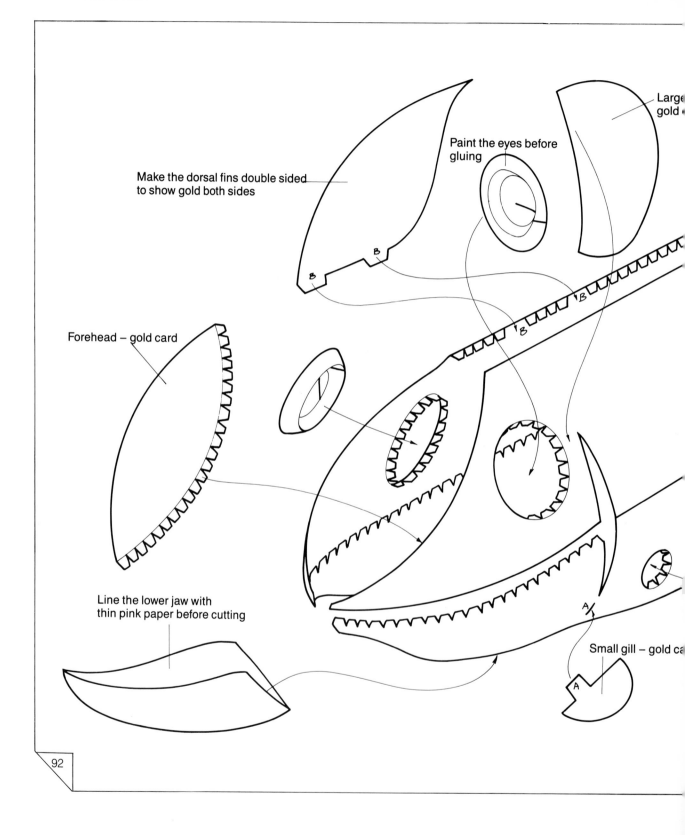

Make the dorsal fins double sided
to show gold both sides

Paint the eyes before
gluing

Large
gold

Forehead – gold card

Line the lower jaw with
thin pink paper before cutting

Small gill – gold ca

92

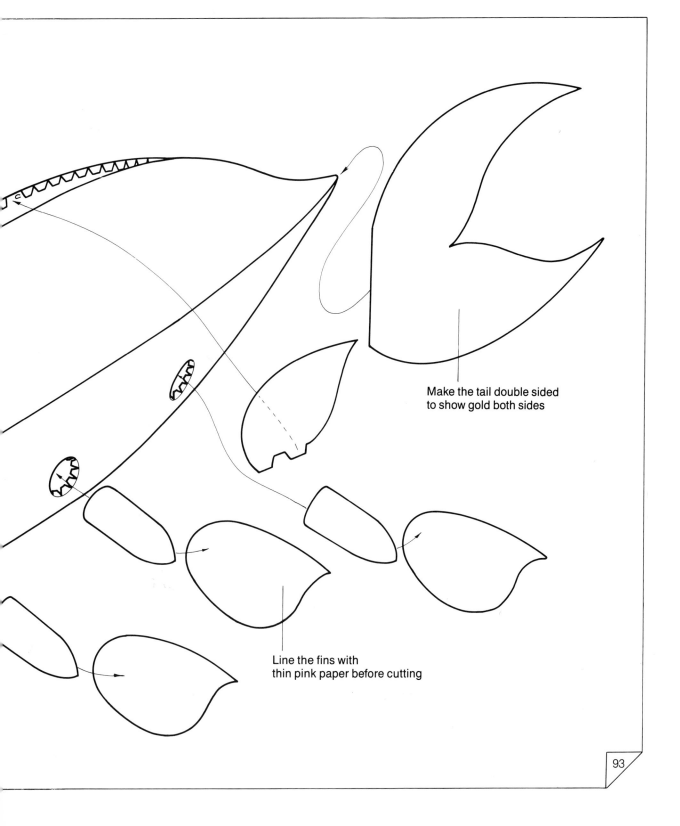

Make the tail double sided
to show gold both sides

Line the fins with
thin pink paper before cutting

Below: Stegosaurus

Above: Eusthenopteron

STEGOSAURUS

The stegosaurids – it means 'roofed reptile' – were notable for the arrangement of large bony plates down their backs. They, like many other dinosaur characteristics, have been the subject of much learned debate; were they arranged in pairs or alternately, did they lie flat over the animal's body or did they stand up, were they for defence, attack, or heat exchange? The last explanation, in view of the fact that examination of fossils has revealed a honeycombed bone structure with a fine 'veined' appearance, seems to be the most likely; a rich blood supply to the plates would have allowed the animal to dissipate or absorb heat when it needed to, regulating its body temperature. Furthermore, even if the plates did lie down over the body, they would still have left large side and belly areas exposed, so the 'protection' theory does not have much to recommend it.

(See colour photograph on page 94.)

YOU WILL NEED
Scalpel or modelling knife
Scissors
Impact adhesive

2 sheets of minimum 16½ × 23⅜in (420 × 594mm) thick orange paper
1 sheet of minimum 16½ × 23⅜in (420 × 594mm) thick yellow paper
1 sheet of minimum 8¼ × 11¾in (210 × 297mm) thin pink paper
1 sheet of minimum 8¼ × 11¾in (210 × 297mm) thick white paper
1 sheet of minimum 11¾ × 16½in (297 × 420mm) thick blue paper
Offcuts of red paper

1 Cut out the two sides of the body from orange paper and the belly from yellow.

2 Glue the two sides of the body together, 1 to **1**.

3 Glue the belly into position, 2 to **2**, 3 to **3**.

4 Cut out the three pieces that make the front leg from orange paper. On the upper leg glue 4 to **4**.

5 On the lower leg glue 5 to **5** to form a ring.

6 Join the upper and lower legs, 6 to **6**.

7 Insert the knee, 7 to **7**.

8 Cut out a foot from orange paper. Pinch and glue 8 to **8**, 9 to **9**, 10 to **10**, 11 to **11**, 12 to **12** and 13 to **13**.

9 Glue the complete foot on to the base of the lower leg, 14 to **14** and 15 to **15**.

10 Glue the finished leg to the body, 16 to **16**.

11 Repeat steps 4–10 using mirror image pieces for the second front leg.

12 Cut out the three pieces that make a back leg from orange paper. Cut out a foot from orange paper.

13 On the upper leg glue 17 to **17** to form a ring.

14 Likewise, on the lower leg glue 18 to **18**.

15 Join the upper and lower legs, 19 to **19**.

16 Insert the knee, 20 to **20**.

17 Repeat the foot process, gluing 8 to **8**, 9 to **9**, 10 to **10**, 11 to **11**, 12 to **12** and 13 to **13**.

18 Glue the finished foot on to the base of the lower leg, 14 to **14**, 15 to **15**.

19 Glue the complete leg into the body, 21 to **21**.

20 Repeat steps 12–19 using mirror image pieces for the second back leg.

21 Cut out the two tail sides from orange paper. Cut the tail base from yellow paper.

22 Glue the two tail sides together, 22 to **22**.

23 Insert the tail base, 23 to **23** and 24 to **24**.

24 Cut out two horns from white paper. Glue them into cone shapes, 25 to **25**, 26 to **26**. Glue the completed horns on to the tail, 27 to **27** and 28 to **28**.

25 Glue the tail on to the body.

26 Before cutting out the upper and lower jaws stick the orange paper on to the thin pink paper. Cut out the upper and lower jaws.

27 On the lower jaw, glue 30 to **30**, and 31 to **31**.

28 On the upper jaw, glue 32 to **32** and 33 to **33**.

29 Glue the upper and lower jaws together, 34 to **34** and 35 to **35**.

30 Cut out the eyes from orange paper. Colour them as indicated in the photograph. Fold them up and glue 36 to **36** on one and 37 to **37** on the other.

31 Cut out the forehead and head back from orange paper.

32 Glue the eyes together, 38 to **38**.

33 Insert and glue the forehead into position, 39 to **39**.

34 Glue the head back into place, 40 to **40**.

35 Glue the complete eye assembly on to the top of the upper jaw by first inserting tab A into slot **A**, then gluing 41 to **41**.

36 Cut out the neck from orange paper. Glue 42 to **42** and 43 to **43**.

37 Glue the neck into the body, 44 to **44**, 45 to **45** and 46 to **46**.

38 Glue the head on to the neck, 47 to **47** and 48 to **48**.

39 Cut out twelve white claws. Glue them together, 49 to **49**, then glue one into each toe hole on each foot, 50 to **50**.

40 Cut out several spade-shaped back plates from blue paper. Slot them into position on the animal's back, tab B to slot **B**; tab C to slot **C** and tab D to slot **D** in the tail.

41 Cut out a tongue from an offcut of red paper. Stick it in position in the mouth, 51 to **51**.

42 Cut out two sets of teeth. Glue one into the upper jaw, 52 to **52**, and one into the lower jaw, 53 to **53**.

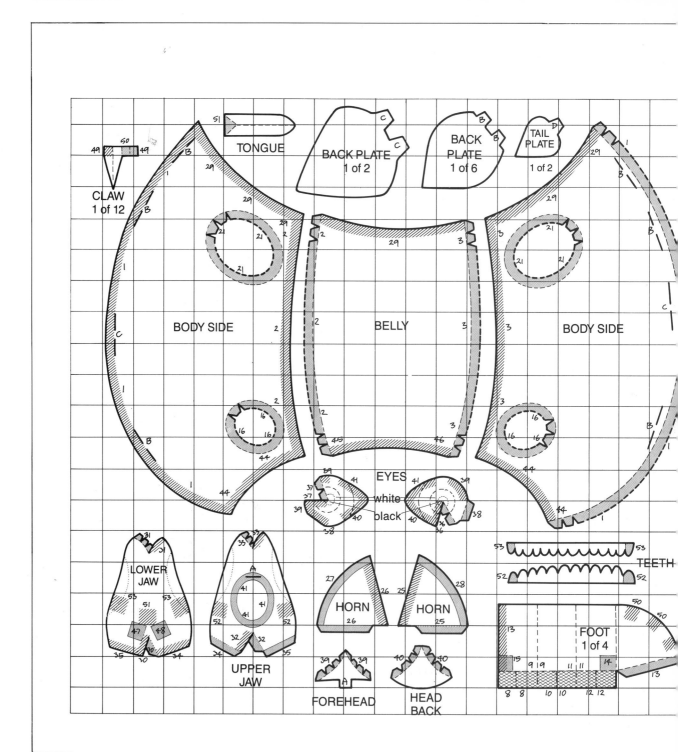

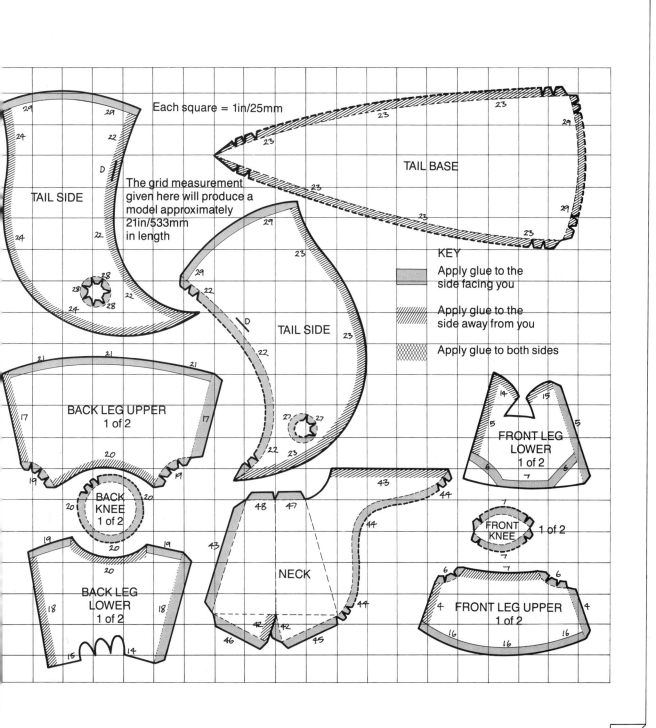

Each square = 1in/25mm

The grid measurement given here will produce a model approximately 21in/533mm in length

TAIL SIDE

TAIL BASE

KEY

Apply glue to the side facing you

Apply glue to the side away from you

Apply glue to both sides

BACK LEG UPPER
1 of 2

TAIL SIDE

FRONT LEG LOWER
1 of 2

BACK KNEE
1 of 2

FRONT KNEE   1 of 2

NECK

BACK LEG LOWER
1 of 2

FRONT LEG UPPER
1 of 2

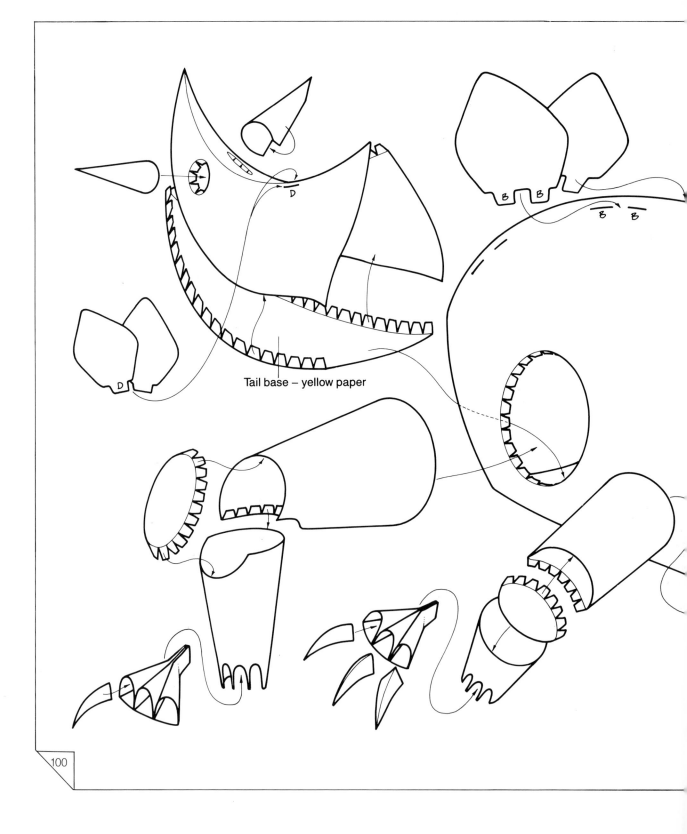

Tail base – yellow paper

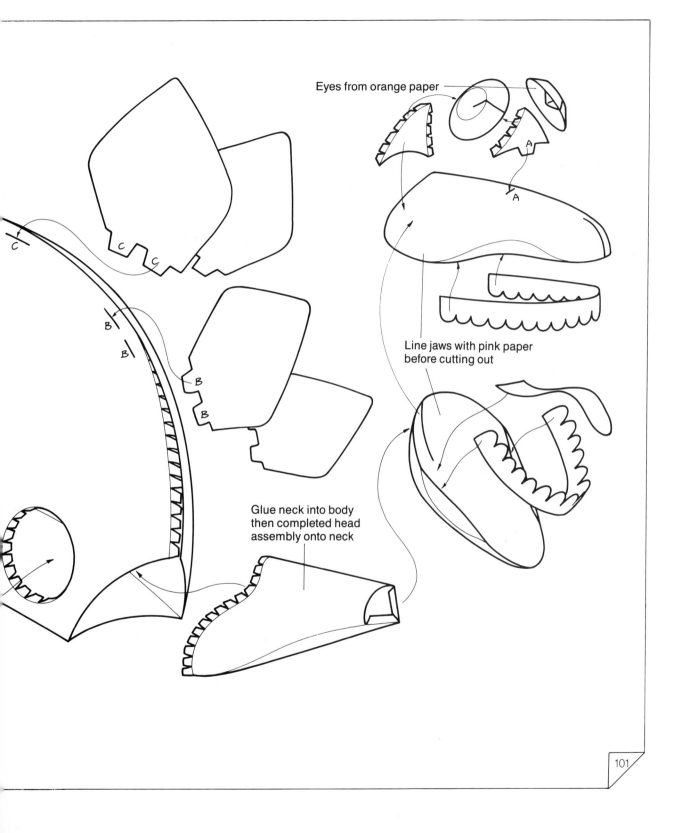

Eyes from orange paper

Line jaws with pink paper
before cutting out

Glue neck into body
then completed head
assembly onto neck

DIMETRODON

Living as it did in the early Permian period (280 million years ago), *Dimetrodon* – 'Two long teeth' – is not technically a dinosaur, but one of the early mammal-like reptiles of the pelycosaur family, the sail reptiles.

Like *Ouranosaurus* and *Stegosaurus*, *Dimetrodon* was distinguished by the huge sail of spines down its back. The generally agreed theory is that they were covered with a large area of skin, richly supplied with blood, which would have acted as a heat-control device for the animal's body operating temperature. Thus it would have been able to absorb the sun's warmth earlier in the day than its competitors for food – *Dimetrodon* was a predator – and could get on the move quicker, to its own advantage. In the heat of the day the sail area would also have allowed it to cool itself more quickly and efficiently.

YOU WILL NEED
Scalpel or modelling knife
Scissors
Impact adhesive

3 sheets of minimum 16½ × 23⅜in (420 × 594mm) thick purple paper
1 sheet of minimum 16½ × 23⅜in (420 × 594mm) thick yellow paper
1 sheet of minimum 11¾ × 16½in (297 × 420mm) thick pink paper
1 sheet of minimum 8¼ × 11¾in (210 × 297mm) thick white paper

1 Cut out the two sides of the body from purple paper and the belly from yellow.

2 Glue the two sides of the body together, 1 to **1**.

3 Insert and glue the belly into place, 2 to **2**.

4 Cut out the three pieces that make a front leg and a foot from purple paper.

5 On the upper piece glue 3 to **3** to form a ring.

6 Likewise, on the lower piece glue 4 to **4**.

7 Join the upper and lower pieces, 5 to **5**.

8 Insert the knee and glue 6 to **6**.

9 Fold up the foot and pinch and glue 7 to **7**, 8 to **8**, 9 to **9**, 10 to **10**, 11 to **11** and 12 to **12**.

10 Glue the foot on to the base of the lower leg, 13 to **13** and 14 to **14**.

11 Glue the leg into the body, 15 to **15**.

12 Repeat steps 4–11 for the second front leg, but use mirror image pieces.

13 Cut out the three pieces that make a back leg and a foot from purple paper.

14 On the upper piece glue 16 to **16**.

15 On the lower piece glue 17 to **17**.

16 Join the upper and lower pieces, 18 to **18**.

17 Insert and glue the knee into position, 19 to **19**.

18 Fold up the foot and pinch and glue 7 to **7**, 8 to **8**, 9 to **9**, 10 to **10**, 11 to **11** and 12 to **12**.

19 Glue the complete foot on to the base of the lower leg, 13 to **13**, 14 to **14**.

20 Stick the complete leg into the body, 20 to **20**.

21 Repeat steps 13–20 using mirror image pieces for the second back leg.

22 Cut out the two sides of the tail from purple paper, and the tail base from yellow paper.

23 Glue the two tail sides together, 21 to **21**.

24 Insert and glue into position the tail base, 22 to **22**, 23 to **23**.

25 Glue the tail on to the body, 24 to **24**.

26 Cut out the neck from purple paper. Glue 25 to **25**.

27 Glue the neck into the body, 26 to **26**, 27 to **27**.

28 Cut out the eye piece, head back, upper and lower jaws from purple paper. Cut out the upper and lower jaw insides from pink paper.

29 On the upper jaw glue 28 to **28**, and 29 to **29**.

30 Glue the upper jaw inside into place, 30 to **30**.

31 On the lower jaw, glue 31 to **31** and 32 to **32**.

32 Glue the lower jaw inside into place, 33 to **33**.

33 Glue the two sides of the head back together, 34 to **34**.

34 Glue 35 to **35** on the head back.

35 Colour the eyes as indicated in the photograph. Fold them up and glue 36 to **36** then 37 to **37**.

36 Glue the eye pieces on to the head back 38 to **38**, 39 to **39**, 40 to **40**.

The paper is folded almost concertina fashion to make the foot with its three claw holes.

37 Glue the upper jaw into place, 41 to **41**, 42 to **42** and 43 to **43**.

38 Now glue the lower jaw into place, 44 to **44**.

39 Glue the complete head on to the neck, 45 to **45**.

40 Cut out twelve white claws, glue them together, 46 to **46**, and stick one into each toe hole on the feet, 47 to **47**.

41 Cut out the crest, decorate it with the yellow spines and slot it into position, slot A to tab **A**, slot D to tab **D**.

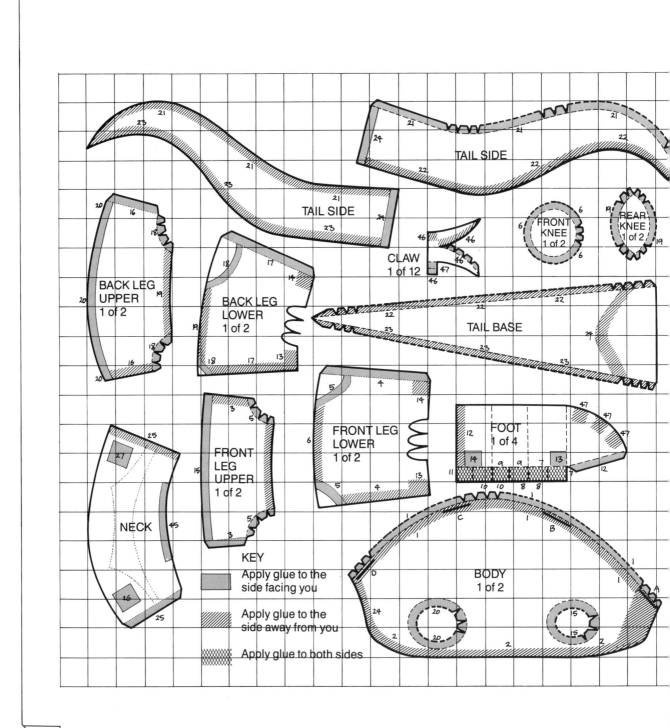

TAIL SIDE

TAIL SIDE

BACK LEG UPPER
1 of 2

BACK LEG LOWER
1 of 2

CLAW
1 of 12

FRONT KNEE
1 of 2

REAR KNEE
1 of 2

TAIL BASE

FRONT LEG LOWER
1 of 2

FOOT
1 of 4

FRONT LEG UPPER
1 of 2

NECK

KEY

Apply glue to the side facing you

Apply glue to the side away from you

Apply glue to both sides

BODY
1 of 2

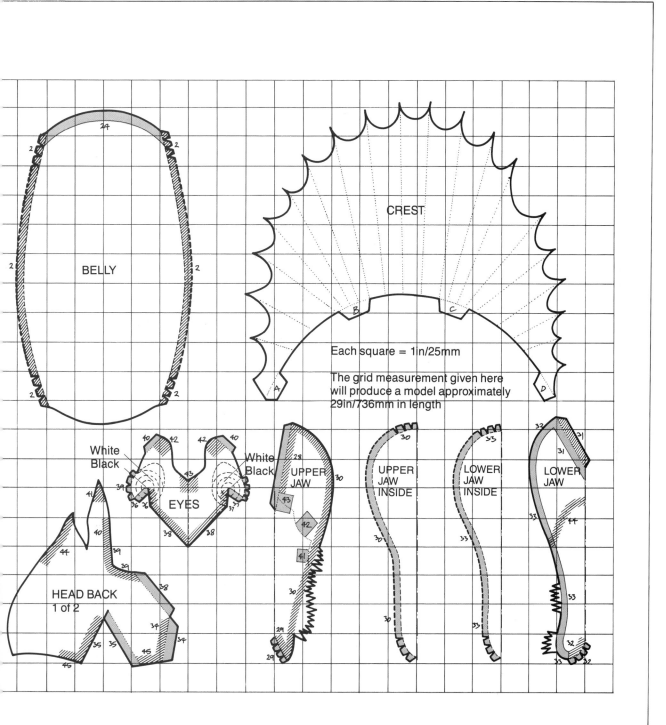

CREST

Each square = 1in/25mm

The grid measurement given here will produce a model approximately 29in/736mm in length

BELLY

White
Black
White
Black

EYES

HEAD BACK
1 of 2

UPPER
JAW

UPPER
JAW
INSIDE

LOWER
JAW
INSIDE

LOWER
JAW

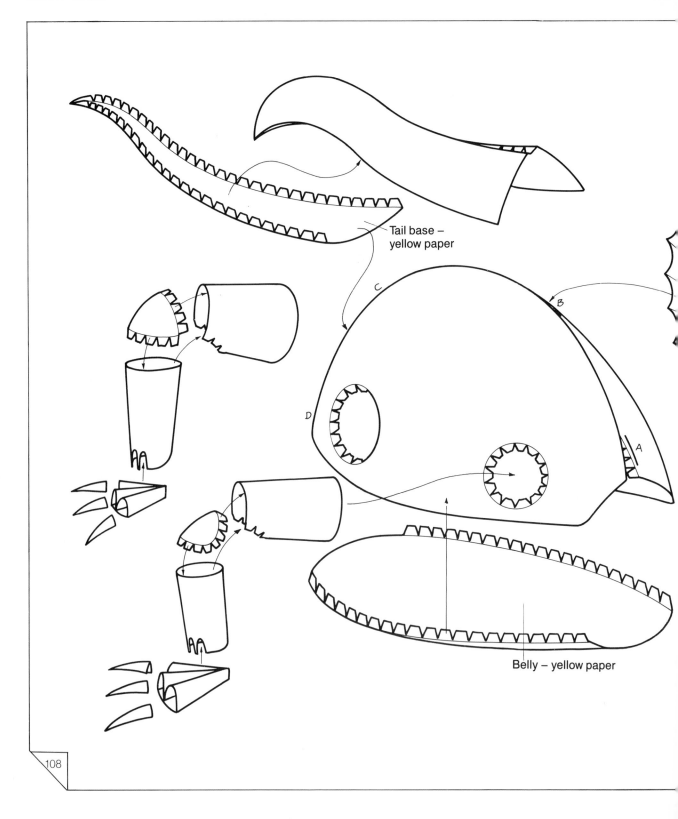

Tail base –
yellow paper

Belly – yellow paper

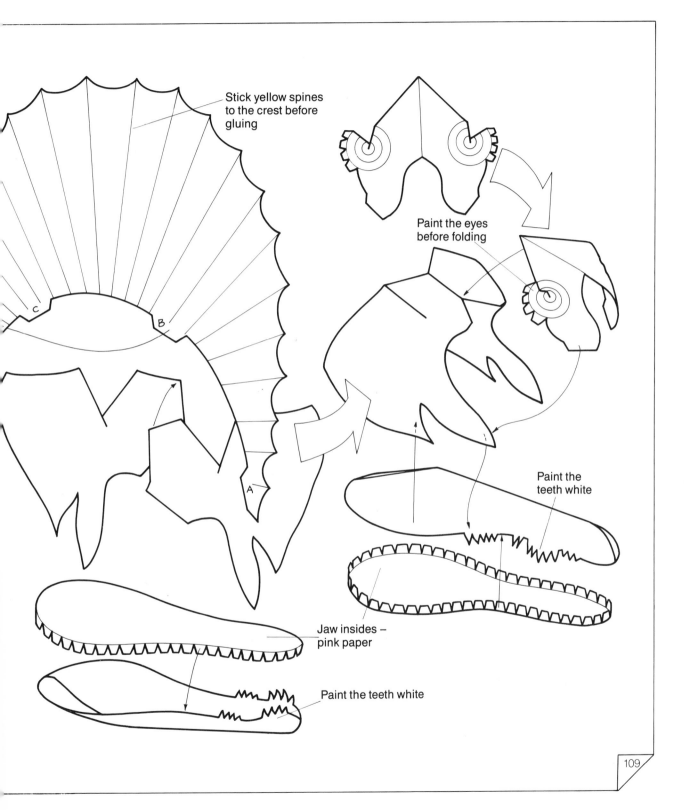

Stick yellow spines to the crest before gluing

Paint the eyes before folding

Paint the teeth white

Jaw insides – pink paper

Paint the teeth white

BARONYX WALKERI

Until very recently (in palaeontological terms) not a lot was known about the dromaeosaurids, a group of medium-sized – up to about 10ft (3m) – flesh-eating dinosaurs. Some significant steps were made towards more understanding of this group in the 1960s, but the biggest dinosaur excitement of the century was created in 1982 by the find in a Surrey claypit of 'The Claw' – a massive talon over 12in (31cm) long round its outside curve. It was taken to the British Museum of Natural History, the site was excavated, and the animal which became popularly known as 'Claws' came to light.

YOU WILL NEED
Scalpel or modelling knife
Scissors
Impact adhesive

3 sheets of minimum 16½×23⅜in (420×594mm) thick red paper
1 sheet of minimum 16½×23⅜in (420×594mm) thick yellow paper
1 sheet of minimum 11¾×16½in (297×420mm) thick pink paper
1 sheet of minimum 8¼×11¾in (210×297mm) thick white paper
1 sheet of minimum 8¼×11¾in (210×297mm) thin pink paper

1 Cut out the two halves of the body from red paper, and the two halves of the belly from yellow paper.

2 On the body glue 1 to **1**.

3 Join both halves of the body, 2 to **2**.

4 Join the two halves of the belly together, 3 to **3**.

5 Glue the complete belly to the body, 4 to **4**.

6 Cut out the five pieces that make the neck from red paper.

7 Glue 5 to **5** on piece 1 to form a ring.

8 Likewise, glue 6 to **6** on piece 2. Join piece 1 to 2 by gluing 7 to **7**.

9 On piece 3, glue 8 to **8**. Join piece 2 to piece 3 by gluing 9 to **9**.

10 Glue 10 to **10** on piece 4. Join piece 3 to piece 4 by gluing 11 to **11**.

11 Glue 12 to **12** on piece 5. Join piece 4 to piece 5 by gluing 13 to **13**.

12 Insert the neck into the body. Glue 14 to **14**.

13 Cut out the three pieces that form a back leg from red paper. Glue 15 to **15** on the upper leg to form a ring.

14 Glue 16 to **16** on the lower leg.

15 Join the upper and lower legs, 17 to **17**.

16 Insert the knee, 18 to **18**.

17 Cut out a foot. Fold it up and glue 19 to **19**, 20 to **20**, 21 to **21**, 22 to **22**, 23 to **23** and 24 to **24**.

18 Stick the foot to the base of the lower leg, 25 to **25** and 26 to **26**.

19 Glue the leg into the body, 27 to **27**.

20 Repeat steps 13–19 for the second leg, but use mirror image pieces.

21 Cut out the two pieces that make an arm, and a hand from red paper. Cover the palm with thin pink paper.

22 Glue 28 to **28** on the upper arm.

23 Glue 29 to **29**, 30 to **30** on the lower arm.

24 Join the upper and lower arms 31 to **31**.

25 Glue 19 to **19**, 20 to **20**, 21 to **21**, 22 to **22**, 23 to **23** and 24 to **24** on the hand.

26 Join the complete hand to the end of the lower arm, 25 to **25** and 26 to **26**.

27 Glue the arm into the body, 27 to **27**.

28 Repeat steps 21–27 for the second arm, using mirror image pieces.

29 Cut out the two sides of the tail from red paper, and the tail base from yellow paper.

30   Glue the two sides together, 28 to **28**.

31   Insert and glue into place the base, 29 to **29**, 30 to **30**.

32   Glue the complete tail to the body, 31 to **31**, 32 to **32** and 33 to **33**.

33   Cut out the forehead, head back, lower and upper jaws from red paper. Note that the jaws have serrated edges which, when painted white, will become the teeth. Cut out upper and lower jaw insides from thick pink paper.

34   Paint the teeth white, and colour the eyes as indicated in the photograph.

35   Glue 34 to **34** on the lower jaw. Glue 35 to **35** on the lower jaw.

36   Glue the lower jaw inside into place, 36 to **36**.

37   Glue 37 to **37** and 38 to **38** on the upper jaw.

38   Glue the upper jaw inside into place, 39 to **39**.

39   Fold up the eye and glue 40 to **40**.

40   Glue the two halves of the head back together, 41 to **41**. Glue 42 to **42** in each case.

41   Glue the eye/forehead into position on the head back, 43 to **43**, 44 to **44** and 45 to **45**.

42   Glue the upper jaw into place in the head back/forehead assembly, 46 to **46**, 47 to **47**.

43   Glue the lower jaw into place to complete the head, 48 to **48**, 49 to **49**.

44   Glue the complete head on to the neck, 50 to **50**.

45   Cut out twelve white claws, glue them together, 51 to **51** and insert one into each toe hole in the hands and feet, 52 to **52**.
On the hands, try to position the claws so that one of them sticks out much further than the others.

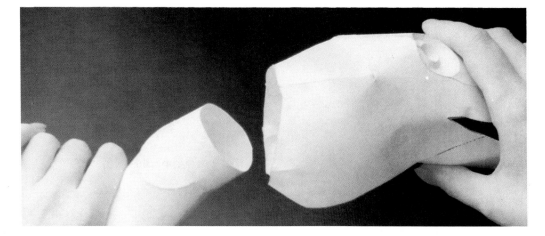

The head is gently lowered on to the neck.

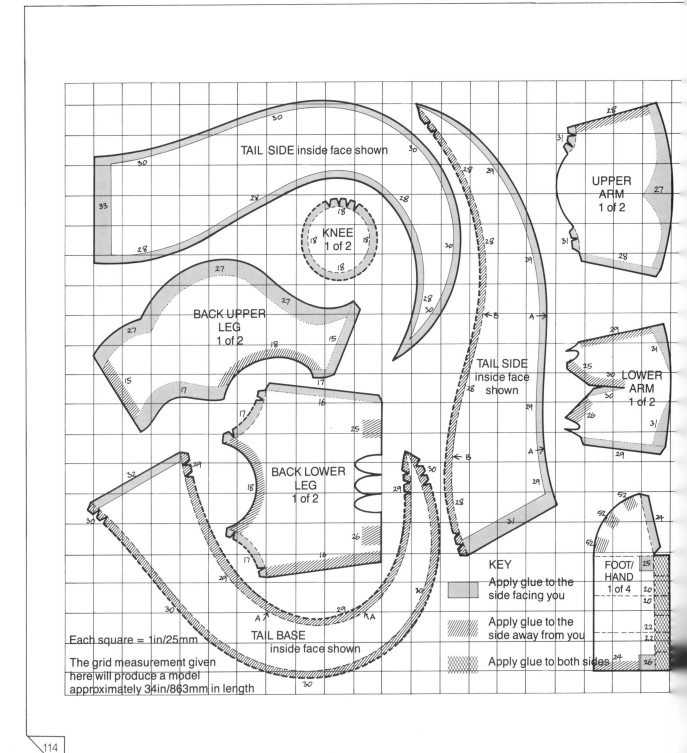

TAIL SIDE inside face shown

KNEE
1 of 2

UPPER
ARM
1 of 2

BACK UPPER
LEG
1 of 2

TAIL SIDE
inside face
shown

LOWER
ARM
1 of 2

BACK LOWER
LEG
1 of 2

FOOT/
HAND
1 of 4

TAIL BASE
inside face shown

Each square = 1in/25mm

The grid measurement given
here will produce a model
approximately 34in/863mm in length

KEY

Apply glue to the
side facing you

Apply glue to the
side away from you

Apply glue to both sides

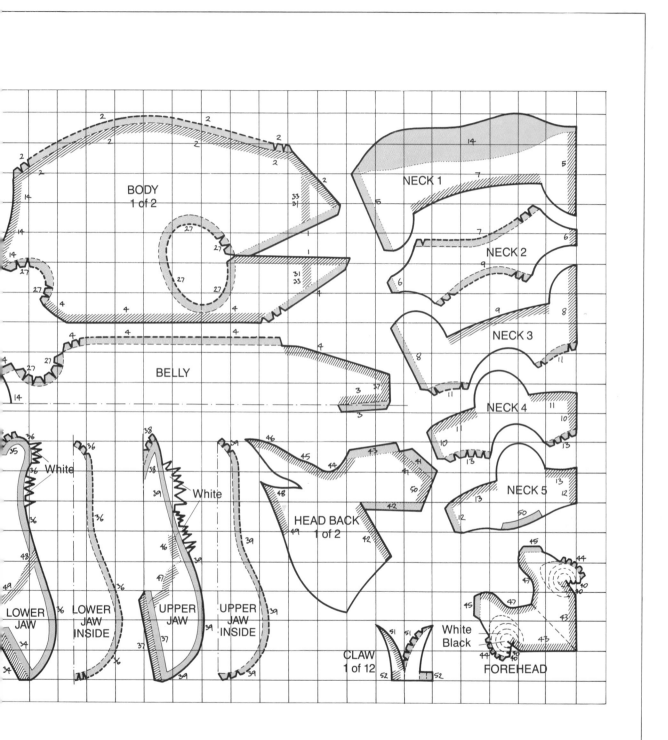

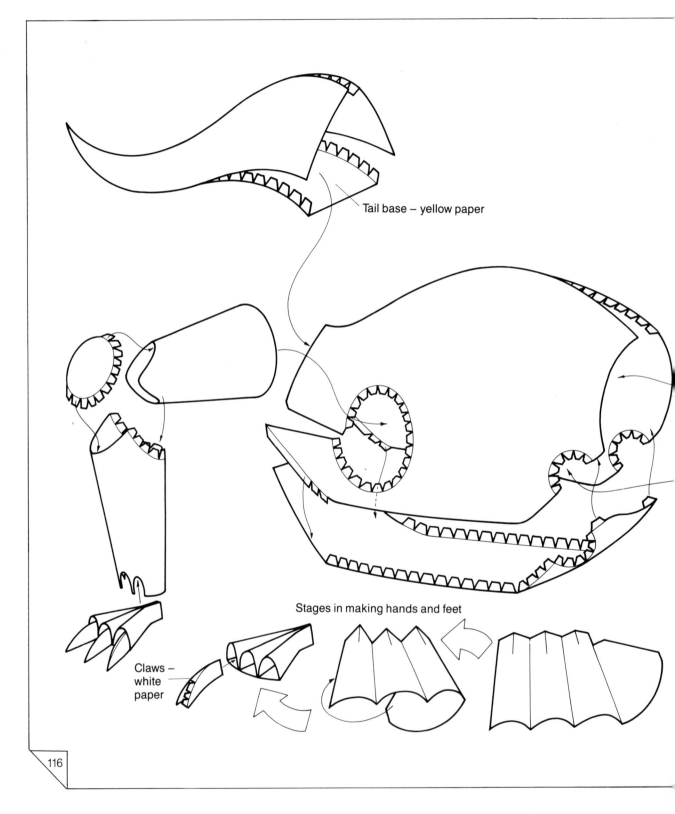

Tail base – yellow paper

Claws –
white
paper

Stages in making hands and feet

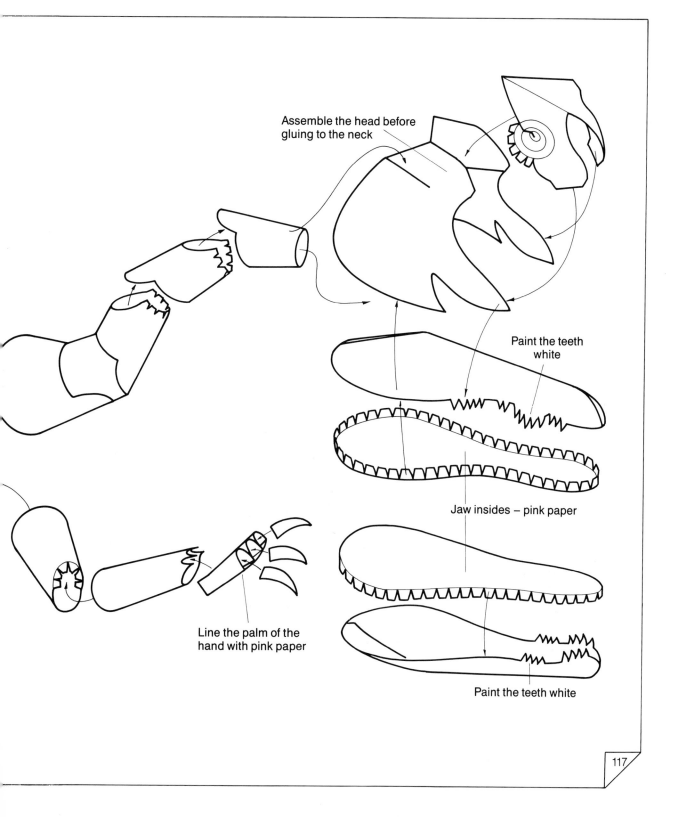

Assemble the head before gluing to the neck

Paint the teeth white

Jaw insides – pink paper

Line the palm of the hand with pink paper

Paint the teeth white

117

DIPLOCAULUS

Living rather before most of the dinosaur inhabitants of this book, *Diplocaulus*, one of the earliest amphibians, was a dweller of the Permian era, about 280 million years ago. It represents a branch in the initial diversification of land dwellers from lobe-finned fish. The peculiar head shield was probably some kind of protection. Other creatures would have found it difficult or impossible to attack or swallow such a spade-like bony structure. An ungainly shape to manoeuvre on land, in the water the head would not have presented so great a hindrance to mobility.

YOU WILL NEED
Scissors
Scalpel or modelling knife
Impact adhesive

3 sheets of minimum 16½×23⅜in (420×594mm) thick marbled paper
1 sheet of minimum 16½×23⅜in (420×594mm) thick yellow paper
1 sheet of minimum 16½×23⅜in (420×594mm) thick orange paper
Offcuts of red paper

1 Cut out two body sections from marbled paper and a belly piece from yellow paper. On each body piece glue A to **A** and B to **B**.

2 Glue the two body pieces together, 1 to **1** along the animal's back.

3 Glue 2 to **2** on the belly piece. Insert the belly and glue 3 to **3**.

4 Cut out the three pieces that make up a front leg from marbled paper.

5 On the upper leg glue 4 to **4**.

6 On the lower leg glue 5 to **5**.

7 Join the upper and lower legs, 6 to **6**.

8 Insert the knee, 7 to **7**.

9 Cut out a foot and glue it into position at the base of the lower leg, 8 to **8**.

10 Cut out the three pieces that make a back leg from marbled paper.

11 On the upper leg glue 9 to **9**.

12 On the lower leg glue 10 to **10**.

13 Join the upper and lower legs 11 to **11**.

14 Insert the knee, 12 to **12**.

15 Cut out a foot and glue it into position at the base of the lower leg, 8 to **8**.

16 Glue the front leg into the body, 14 to **14**.

17 Glue the back leg into the body, 15 to **15**. Repeat steps 4–16 for the remaining legs, using mirror image pieces.

18 Cut out the four pieces that make the head from marbled paper:

a) Head upper piece;
b) Head lower piece;
c) 2×head section 2.

19 Glue 16 to **16** on the upper and lower head pieces.

20 Join the upper and lower head pieces, 17 to **17**.

21 At the back of the head, glue head section 2 into position, 18 to **18**. Repeat for the other side of the head with a mirror image piece.

22 Cut out the two pieces that make the elongated eye sockets.

23 Glue piece 1 into the hole in the head, 19 to **19**.

24 Glue piece 2 into position above piece 1, 20 to **20**.

25 Cut out an eye and colour as indicated. Glue 21 to **21**.

26 Glue the eye on to the eye socket, 22 to **22**.

27 Repeat instructions 22–26 for the remaining eye socket.

28 Cut out a mouth from red paper and glue it in the centre of the lower head.

29 Glue the head to the body, 23 to **23**.

30 Cut out the pattern shapes from orange and yellow paper. Stick them along the back and head to complete this model.

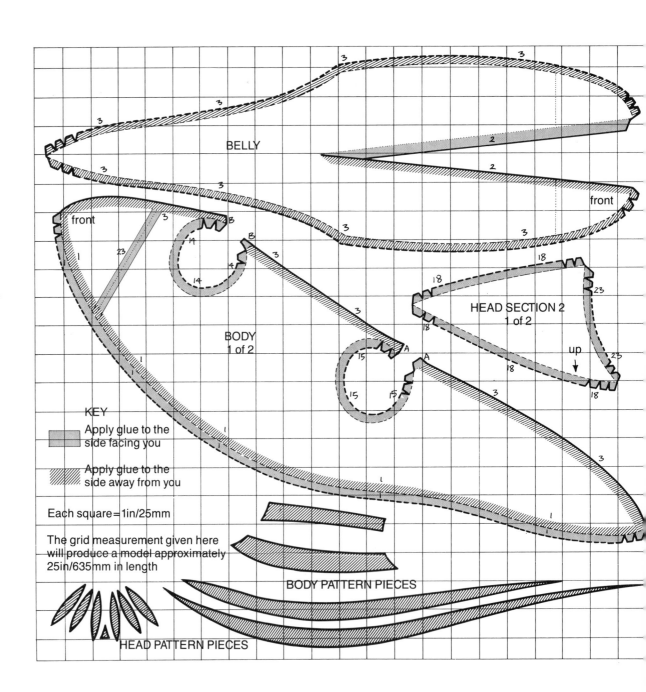

BELLY

front

front

BODY
1 of 2

HEAD SECTION 2
1 of 2

up

KEY

Apply glue to the
side facing you

Apply glue to the
side away from you

Each square=1in/25mm

The grid measurement given here
will produce a model approximately
25in/635mm in length

BODY PATTERN PIECES

HEAD PATTERN PIECES

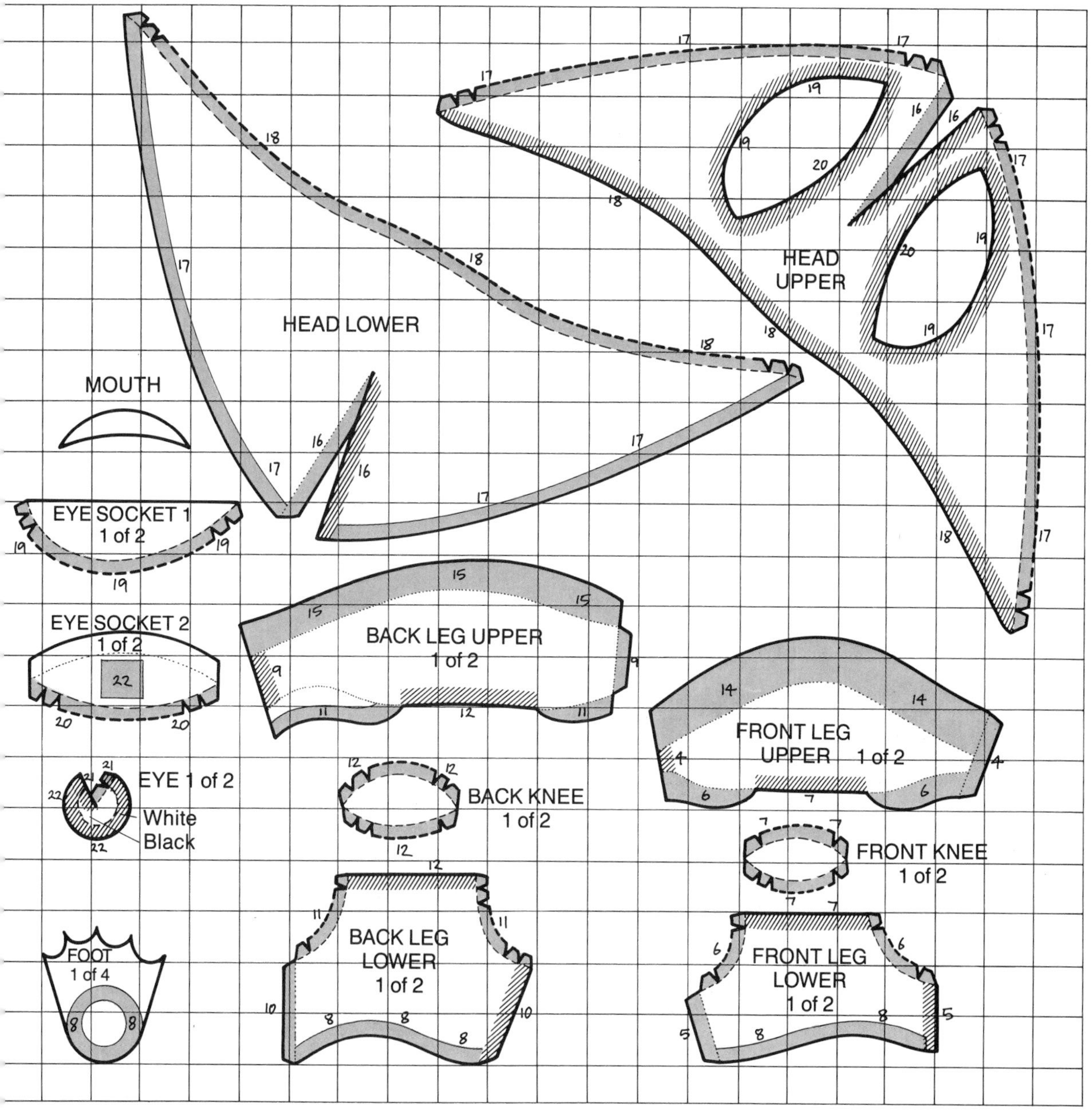

MOUTH

HEAD LOWER

HEAD UPPER

EYE SOCKET 1
1 of 2

EYE SOCKET 2
1 of 2

22

EYE 1 of 2
White
Black

BACK LEG UPPER
1 of 2

FRONT LEG
UPPER   1 of 2

BACK KNEE
1 of 2

FRONT KNEE
1 of 2

FOOT
1 of 4

BACK LEG
LOWER
1 of 2

FRONT LEG
LOWER
1 of 2

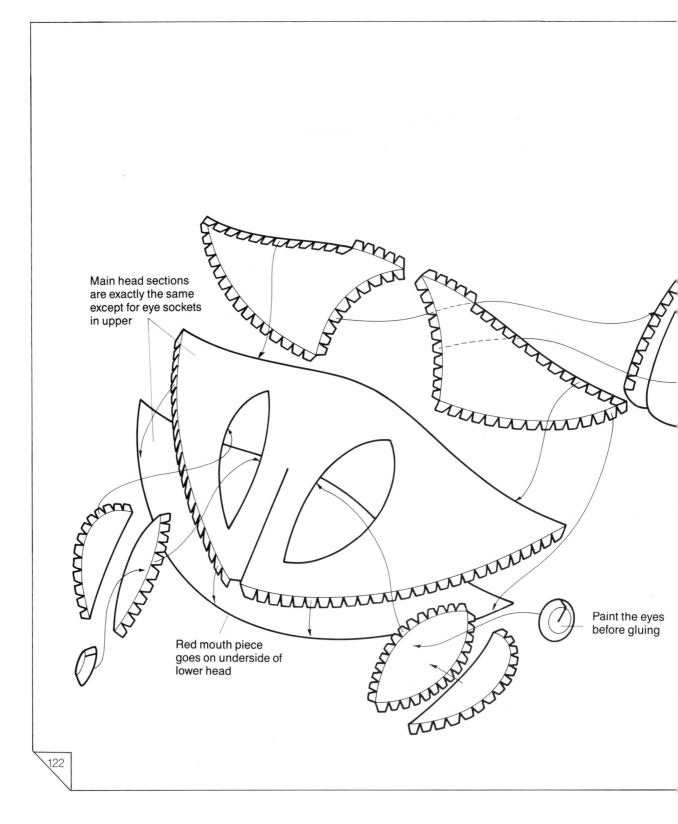

Main head sections
are exactly the same
except for eye sockets
in upper

Red mouth piece
goes on underside of
lower head

Paint the eyes
before gluing

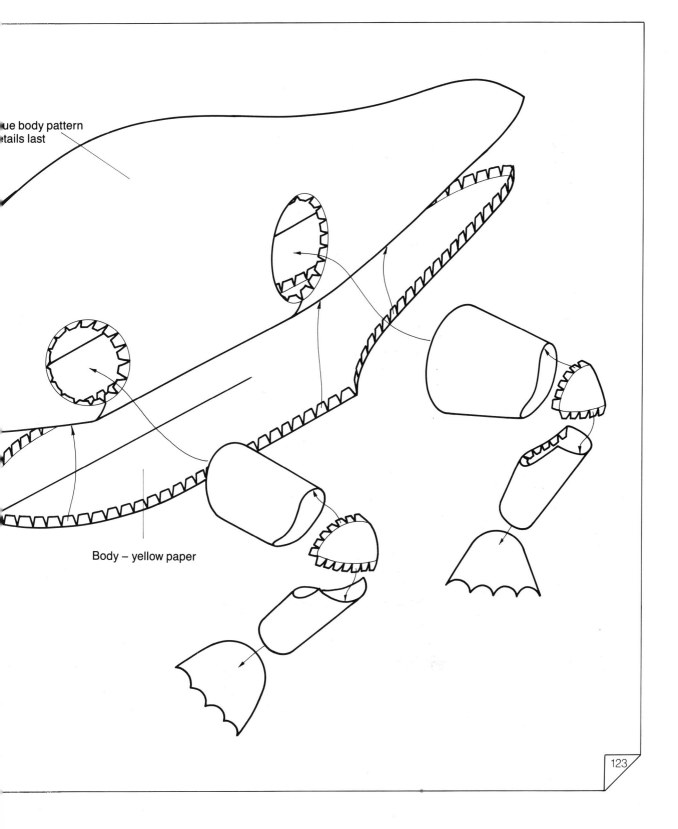

ue body pattern
tails last

Body – yellow paper

KUEHNEOSAURUS

The *Kuehneosaurus* (Küehne's reptile) was discovered in Britain in the late Triassic period 210–200 million years ago. Its existence represents a step in evolution towards the conquest of the air. The creature had enormously long membrane-covered ribs projecting from its sides, which allowed it to glide from tree to tree. 'Gliding lizards' still exist in Malaysia today – and the *Kuehneosaurus* was definitely an early form of lizard, with its limbs splayed outwards and distinctive skull bone structure. It could glide quite considerable distances with little loss of height.

(See colour photograph at the foot of pages 138–139.)

YOU WILL NEED
Scalpel or modelling knife
Scissors
Impact adhesive

1 sheet of minimum 16½ × 23⅜in (420 × 594mm) thick bright blue paper
1 sheet of minimum 16½ × 23⅜in (420 × 594mm) thick yellow paper
1 sheet of minimum 11¾ × 16½in (297 × 420mm) thin pink paper
1 sheet of minimum 8¼ × 11¾in (210 × 297mm) thick white paper
1 sheet of minimum 8¼ × 11¾in (210 × 297mm) thick pink paper
Offcuts of red paper

1 Cut out the four body pieces, the top sections from blue paper, the bottom pieces from yellow.

2 On the top pieces, glue 1 to **1**.

3 On the bottom pieces, glue 2 to **2**.

4 Join the top to the bottom 3 to **3**.

5 Cut out the two tail pieces from blue paper.

6 Score and fold the tail pieces as shown.

7 Glue the two tail pieces together, 4 to **4**, 5 to **5**.

8 Glue the tail to the body, 6 to **6**.

9 Cut out the four pieces that form the arm. Before cutting the hand, glue the blue paper to thin pink paper, so the palm of the hand will be pink.

10 Glue the upper arm, 7 to **7**.

11 Glue the lower arm, 8 to **8**.

12 Join the upper and lower arm, 9 to **9**.

13 Insert the elbow, 10 to **10**.

14 Glue the arm to the body, 11 to **11**.

15 Glue the hand to the arm, 12 to **12**.

16 Cut out the four pieces that form the leg, remembering to stick the blue paper foot on to the thin pink paper in the same way as the hand.

17 Glue 13 to **13** on the upper leg.

18 Glue 14 to **14** on the lower leg.

19 Join the upper and lower legs, 15 to **15**.

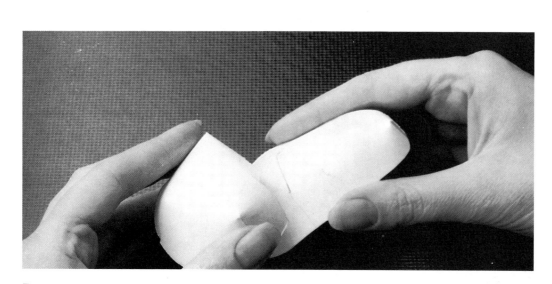

The model's brow has to be slotted into the lower jaw.

20 Insert the knee, 16 to **16**.

21 Glue the leg to the body, 17 to **17**.

22 Glue the foot into position, 18 to **18**.

23 Repeat steps 9–22 using mirror image pieces for the remaining arm and leg.

24 Before cutting out the 'wings', stick the blue paper to the thin pink paper.

25 Cut out the 'wings' and slot them into position between the arms/legs. Tab A to slot **A**, tab B to slot **B**, and in the body, tab C to slot **C**.

26 Repeat this for the second 'wing'.

27 Cut out the four head pieces:
a) Upper jaw from blue
b) Lower jaw from blue (stuck to thin pink paper)
c) Forehead from blue
d) Upper jaw inside from thick pink paper.

28 On the upper jaw stick 19 to **19**, 20 to **20**.

29 On the lower jaw stick 21 to **21**, 22 to **22**.

30 Stick the 'upper jaw inside' into the upper jaw, 23 to **23**.

31 Take the forehead and glue 24 to **24**, 25 to **25** and 26 to **26**.

32 Join the forehead to the upper jaw. Slot tab D into slot **D** and glue 27 to **27**.

33 Cut out two pink eyes and tack them on to the forehead 28 to **28**. (They can be cut with a hole punch.)

34 Glue the head on to the body, 29 to **29** and 30 to **30**.

35 Cut out the teeth from white paper.

36 Glue the upper teeth into the upper jaw, 31 to **31**, and the lower teeth into the lower jaw, 32 to **32**.

37 Cut out the tongue from red paper and stick it at the back of the lower jaw, 33 to **33**.

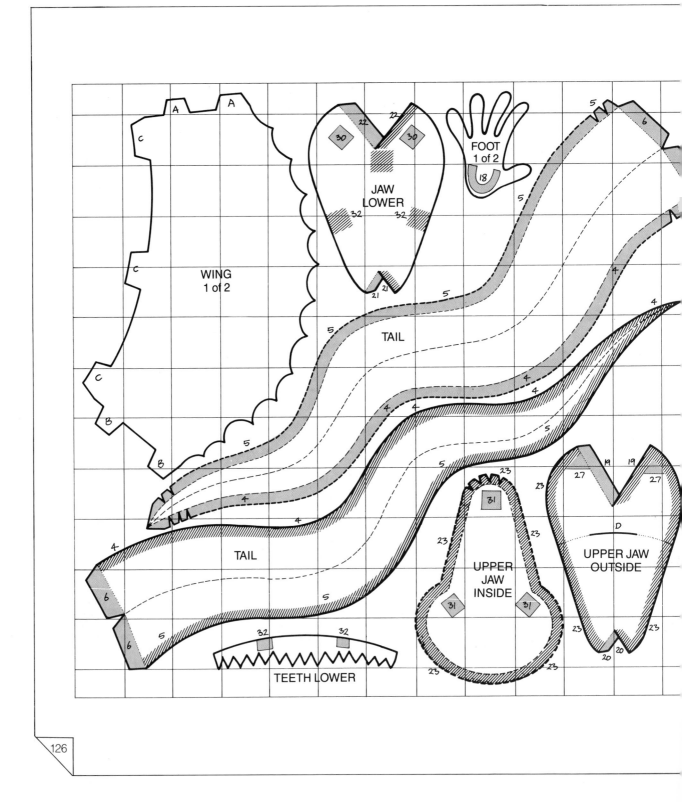

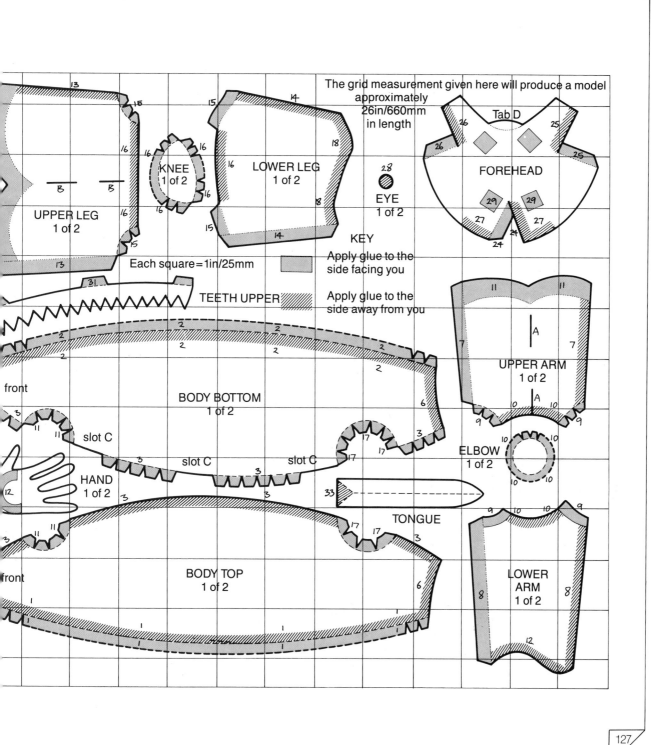

The grid measurement given here will produce a model approximately 26in/660mm in length

UPPER LEG
1 of 2

KNEE
1 of 2

LOWER LEG
1 of 2

EYE
1 of 2

FOREHEAD

Tab D

Each square = 1in/25mm

TEETH UPPER

KEY

Apply glue to the side facing you

Apply glue to the side away from you

UPPER ARM
1 of 2

front

BODY BOTTOM
1 of 2

slot C

slot C

slot C

ELBOW
1 of 2

HAND
1 of 2

TONGUE

LOWER
ARM
1 of 2

front

BODY TOP
1 of 2

127

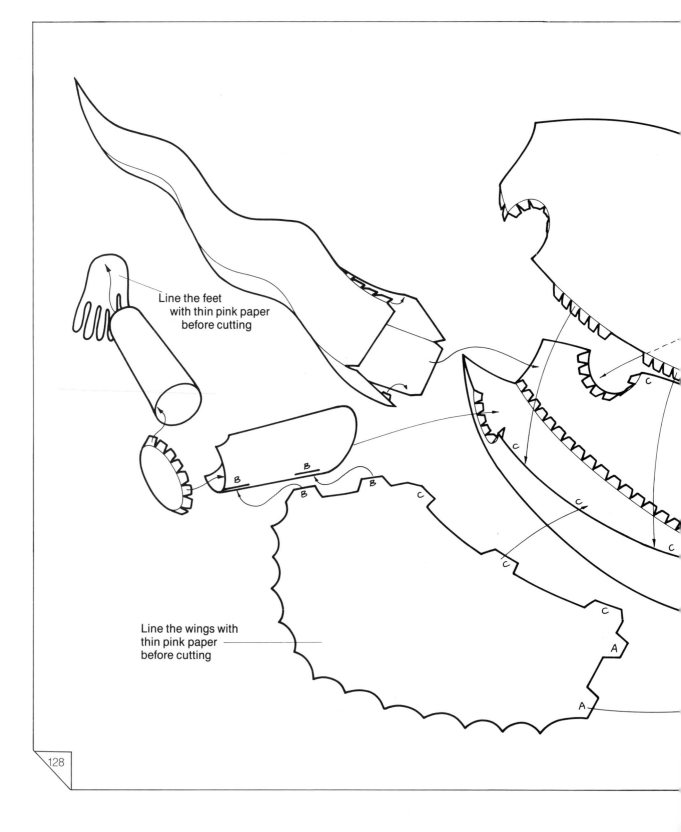

Line the feet
with thin pink paper
before cutting

Line the wings with
thin pink paper
before cutting

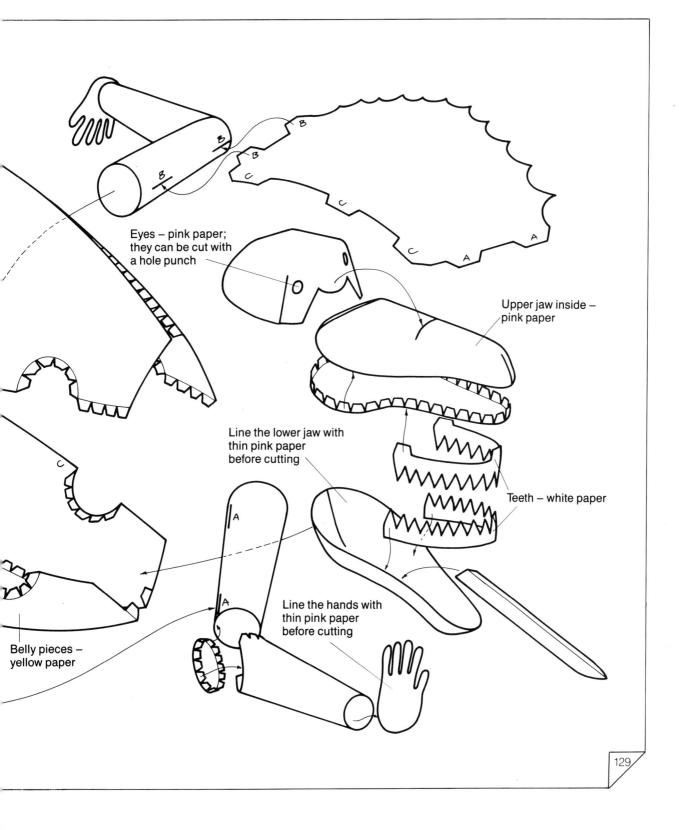

Eyes – pink paper;
they can be cut with
a hole punch

Upper jaw inside –
pink paper

Line the lower jaw with
thin pink paper
before cutting

Teeth – white paper

Belly pieces –
yellow paper

Line the hands with
thin pink paper
before cutting

BRONTOSAURUS/ APATOSAURUS

As familiar an image of a dinosaur as any could be, the long-necked, long-tailed *Brontosaurus* (more correctly *Apatosaurus*) was among the largest of the dinosaurs, extending in some cases to 88ft (26.80m) long! 'Brontosaurus' is in fact rather like a 'pet name', meaning 'Thunder reptile' or 'Deceptive reptile', a product of the confusion and rivalry among the palaeontologists who were first researching these creatures in the 1880s. 'Deceptive reptile' is an appropriate name; many reconstructed skeletons have feet from other branches of the family.

(See colour photograph at the foot of pages 138–139.)

YOU WILL NEED
Scalpel or modelling knife
Scissors
Impact adhesive

4 sheets of minimum 16½×23⅜in (420×594mm) thick pink paper
1 sheet of minimum 11¾×16½in (297×420mm) medium blue paper
1 sheet of minimum 11¾×16½in (297×420mm) medium white paper
1 sheet of minimum 8¼×11¾in (210×297mm) thin pale pink paper
Offcuts of red paper

1 Cut out the body from thick pink paper.

2 Glue 1 to **1** and 2 to **2**.

3 Glue 3 to **3** and 4 to **4**.

4 Glue 5 to **5**.

5 Cut out the nine pieces that form the tail from thick pink paper.

6 Glue 6 to **6** on piece 1 and 7 to **7** on piece 2. Join piece 1 to 2 by gluing 8 to **8**.

7 Glue 10 to **10** on piece 3. Join piece 2 to 3 by gluing 9 to **9**.

8 Glue 11 to **11** on piece 4. Join piece 3 to 4 by gluing 12 to **12**.

9 Glue 13 to **13** on piece 5. Join piece 4 to 5 by gluing 14 to **14**.

10 Glue 15 to **15** on piece 6. Join piece 5 to 6 by gluing 16 to **16**.

11 Glue 17 to **17** on piece 7. Join piece 6 to 7 by gluing 18 to **18**.

12 Glue 19 to **19** on piece 8. Join piece 7 to 8 by gluing 20 to **20**.

13 Glue 21 to **21** on piece 9, the tail tip. Join piece 8 to 9 by gluing 22 to **22**.

14 For the neck repeat instructions 5–12.

15 Glue the tail to the body 22 to **22**.

16 Glue the neck to the body 23 to **23**.

17 Cut out the three pieces that form a front leg from thick pink paper.

18 Glue 24 to **24** on the upper leg.

19 Glue 25 to **25** on the lower leg.

20 Join the upper and lower leg 26 to **26**.

21 Insert the knee 27 to **27**.

22 Cut out the three pieces that form a back leg from thick pink paper.

23 Glue 28 to **28** on the upper leg.

24 Glue 29 to **29** on the lower leg.

25 Join the upper and lower leg 30 to **30**.

26 Insert the knee 31 to **31**.

27 Repeat steps 17–26 using mirror image pieces to make the remaining legs.

28 Glue the front leg into position 32 to **32**.

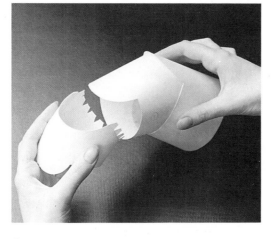

One ringed section of neck is fitted into another. The same principle is used on the tail.

29 Glue the back leg into position 33 to **33**.

30 Before cutting out the two pieces that form the head, glue them on to thin pale pink paper (so that the inside of the mouth will be a different colour to the rest of the dinosaur).

31 Cut out the two pieces that form the head.

32 Glue 34 to **34** on the upper piece.

33 Glue 35 to **35** on the upper piece.

34 Glue 36 to **36** on the lower piece.

35 Glue 37 to **37** on the lower piece.

36 Join the upper and lower pieces 38 to **38**.

37 Before making up the eyes, paint where indicated to give the model a cross-eyed stare.

38 Fold up the eyes 39 to **39** and 40 to **40**.

39 Insert each eye into the head 41 to **41** and 42 to **42**.

40 Cut out the teeth from white paper.

41 Insert the teeth 43 to **43** in the upper jaw; 44 to **44** in the lower jaw.

42 Join the head to the neck 45 to **45**.

43 Cut out some 'toenails' from white paper and stick them to the end of each leg 46 to **46**.

44 Cut out several blue circle details and randomly place them on the completed brontosaurus.

45 Cut out the tongue from red paper and position it in the model's mouth.

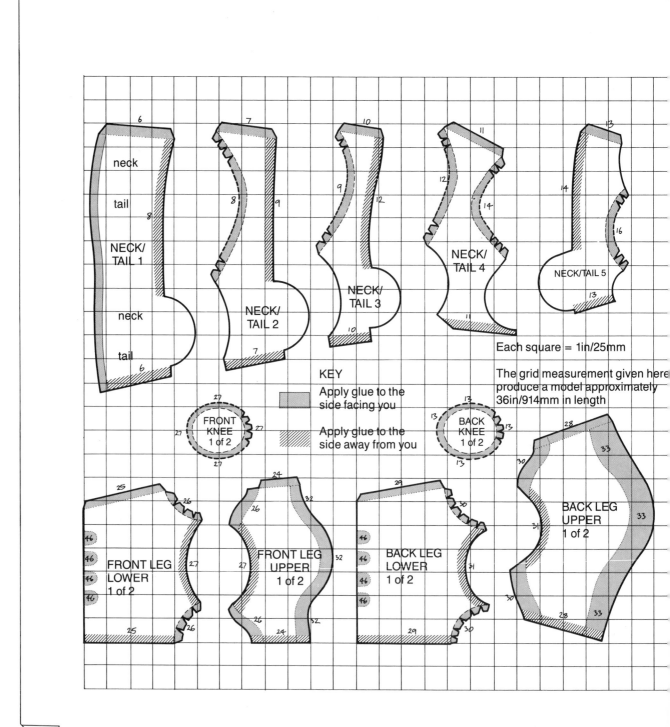

neck

tail

NECK/
TAIL 1

neck

tail

NECK/
TAIL 2

NECK/
TAIL 3

NECK/
TAIL 4

NECK/TAIL 5

Each square = 1in/25mm

The grid measurement given here
produce a model approximately
36in/914mm in length

KEY

Apply glue to the
side facing you

Apply glue to the
side away from you

FRONT
KNEE
1 of 2

BACK
KNEE
1 of 2

FRONT LEG
LOWER
1 of 2

FRONT LEG
UPPER
1 of 2

BACK LEG
LOWER
1 of 2

BACK LEG
UPPER
1 of 2

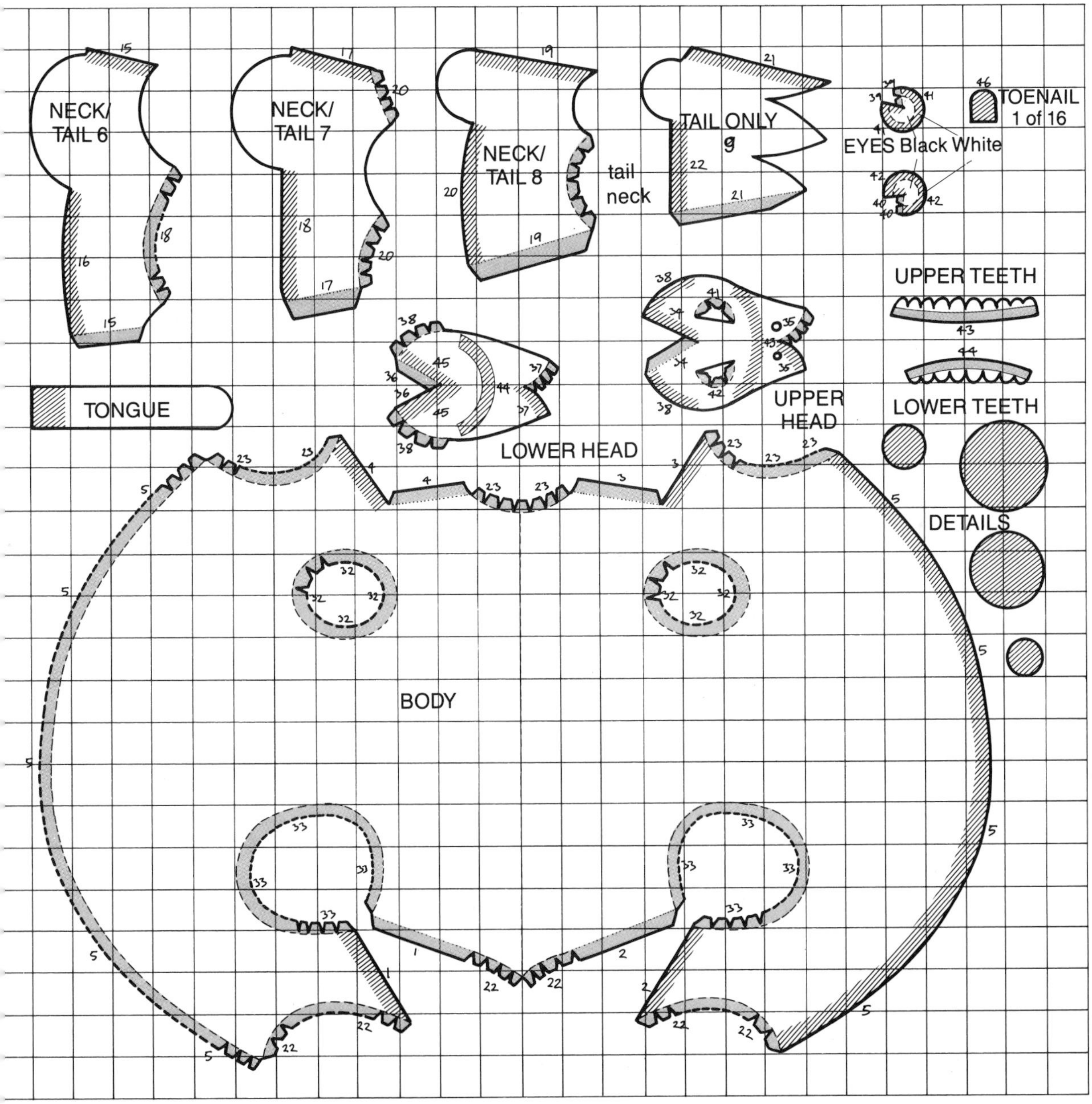

NECK/TAIL 6

NECK/TAIL 7

NECK/TAIL 8

tail
neck

TAIL ONLY
g

TOENAIL
1 of 16

EYES Black White

UPPER TEETH

TONGUE

LOWER HEAD

UPPER
HEAD

LOWER TEETH

DETAILS

BODY

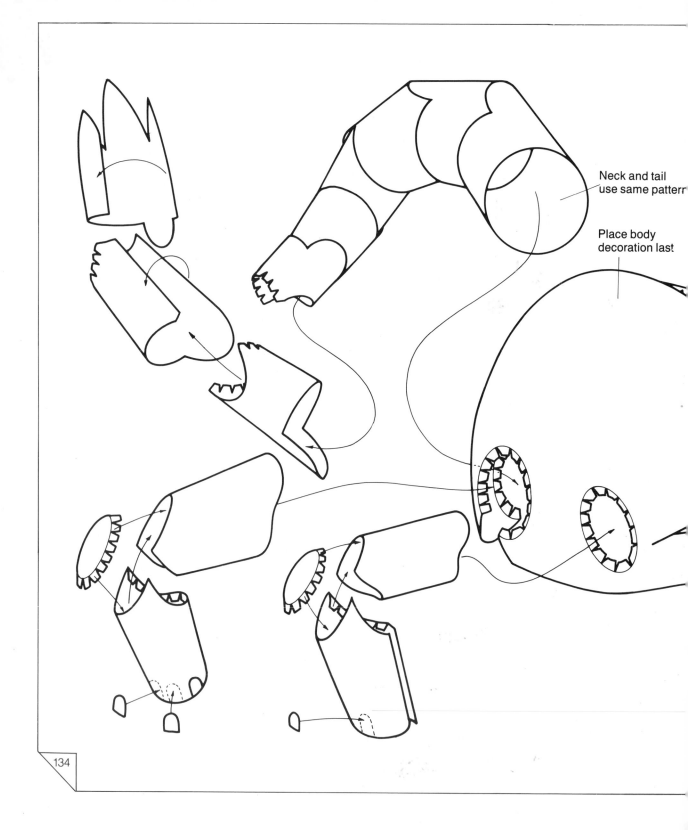

Neck and tail
use same pattern

Place body
decoration last

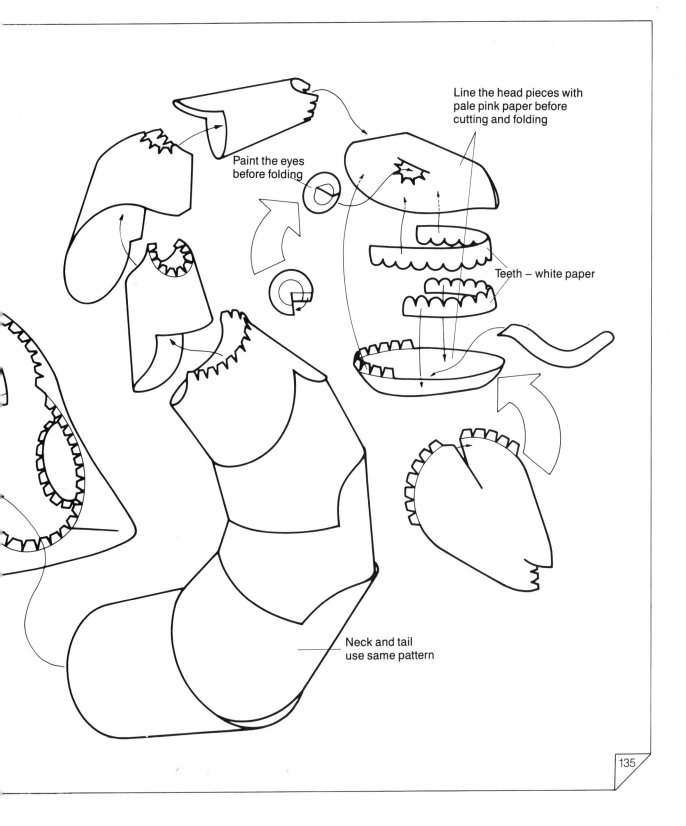

Line the head pieces with
pale pink paper before
cutting and folding

Paint the eyes
before folding

Teeth – white paper

Neck and tail
use same pattern

ARCHELON

Like many of the animals in this book, *Archelon* – the giant turtle – is not strictly a dinosaur. It was a contemporary, however, and is bound to have populated the ancient seas at the time massive reptiles were fighting it out on land. Curiously, turtle fossils seem to be either skulls or shells, but rarely have the two been found together.

Archelon lived during the Cretaceous period, 135 million years ago. It grew to 12ft (3.6m) in length, and had enormous flippers, which suggest a respectable turn of aquatic speed. The shell was well developed – a necessity, in view of the variety and ferocity of marine predators of the time.

Archelon had large eyes for seeing in the murky deep, and a huge, powerful hooked beak, which indicates that its main diet was probably shellfish. It doubtless lived in much the same way as do the turtles of today, swimming for long distances under water and returning to land to lay its eggs in the sand.

(See colour photograph at the top of page 139.)

YOU WILL NEED
Scalpel or modelling knife
Scissors
Impact adhesive

1 sheet of minimum 16½×23⅜in (420×594mm) thick purple paper
1 sheet of minimum 16½×23⅜in (420×594mm) thick pale grey paper
1 sheet of minimum 16½×23⅜in (420×594mm) thick orange paper
1 sheet of minimum 8¼×11¾in (210×297mm) thick pink paper
1 sheet of minimum 8¼×11¾in (210×297mm) thin pink paper
1 sheet of minimum 11¾×16½in (297×420mm) gold foil or card
Offcuts of red paper

1 Cut out an upper shell from purple paper.

2 Glue 1 to **1**, 2 to **2**, 3 to **3**, 4 to **4**, 5 to **5**, 6 to **6**, 7 to **7** and 8 to **8**.

3 Cut out a lower shell from pale grey paper.

4 Glue 9 to **9**, 10 to **10**, 11 to **11**, 12 to **12**, 13 to **13**, 14 to **14**, 15 to **15**, 16 to **16**, 17 to **17** and 18 to **18**.

5 Join the upper and lower shells together. The lower shell is shown with the 'underside' facing you, so fold 'away' from you and flip it underneath the upper shell. The folded edges should show the neatest join outside. Thus join 19 to **19**, 20 to **20**, 21 to **21**, 22 to **22**, 23, to **23**, 24 to **24**, 25 to **25**, 26 to **26**, 27 to **27** and 28 to **28**.

6 Cut out the four head pieces:
a) Upper jaw – orange
b) Lower jaw – orange stuck to thin pink
c) Palate – thick pink
d) Forehead – orange

7 On the upper jaw glue 29 to **29** and 30 to **30**.

8 Insert and glue the forehead, 31 to **31** and 32 to **32**.

9 Glue the palate into the upper jaw, 33 to **33**.

10 On the lower jaw glue 34 to **34**.

11 Cut out two eyes and colour as indicated in the photograph.

12 Fold them up and glue 35 to **35**.

13 Stick them into position on the head, 36 to **36**. Join the upper and lower jaws, 37 to **37**.

14 Cut out a neck from orange paper. Glue 38 to **38**.

15 Glue the head into position on the neck, 39 to **39**, 40 to **40**.

16 Stick the head/neck assembly into the shell, 41 to **41**.

17 Cut out a front arm, but before cutting the adjoining fin stick the orange paper to thin pink paper.

18 Glue 42 to **42** on the arm.

19 Glue 43 to **43** on the fin.

20 Stick the fin to the arm, 44 to **44**.

21 Join the complete fin/arm section to the shell, 45 to **45**.

22 Cut out a back arm. Before cutting out the fin stick the orange paper to thin pink.

23 On the arm glue 46 to **46**.

24 On the fin glue 47 to **47**.

25 Glue the fin to the arm, 48 to **48**.

26 Stick the complete piece into the body, 49 to **49**.

27 Repeat steps 17–26 with mirror image pieces for the other fins.

28 Cut out the shell decorations from gold foil or card. Stick them into position on the shell, 50 to **50**, 51 to **51**, 52 to **52**, 53 to **53**, 54 to **54**, 55 to **55**, 56 to **56**, 57 to **57**, 58 to **58**, 59 to **59**, 60 to **60**, 61 to **61** and 62 to **62**.

29 Cut out a tongue from red paper and position it in the model's mouth.

The turtle's jaw is glued into its head.

Above: Kuehneosaurus
Above right: Archelon
Right: Brontosaurus/Apatosaurus

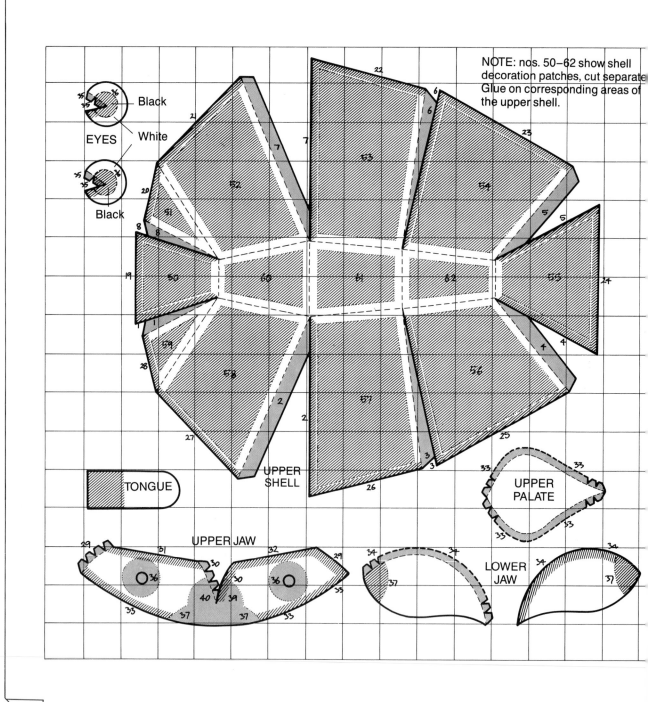

EYES

Black

White

Black

NOTE: nos. 50–62 show shell decoration patches, cut separate. Glue on corresponding areas of the upper shell.

TONGUE

UPPER SHELL

UPPER JAW

UPPER PALATE

LOWER JAW

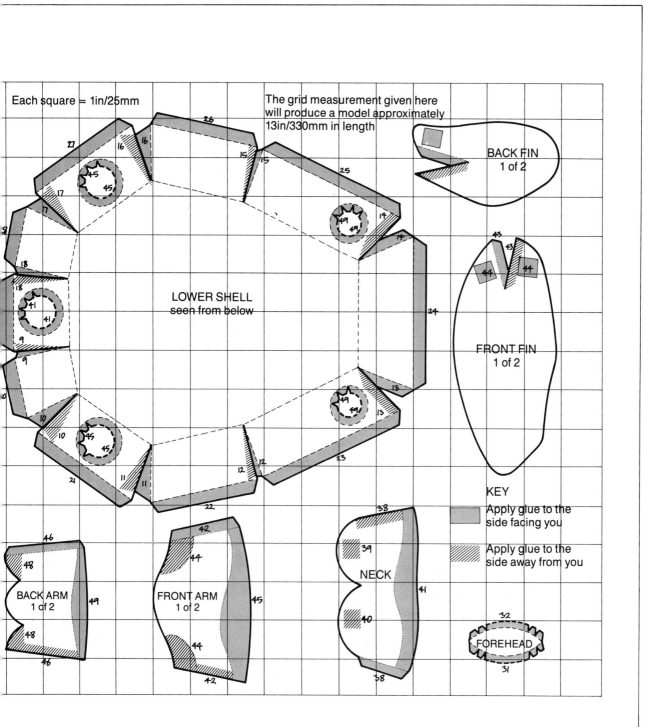

Each square = 1in/25mm

The grid measurement given here will produce a model approximately 13in/330mm in length

BACK FIN
1 of 2

LOWER SHELL
seen from below

FRONT FIN
1 of 2

KEY

Apply glue to the side facing you

Apply glue to the side away from you

NECK

BACK ARM
1 of 2

FRONT ARM
1 of 2

FOREHEAD

141

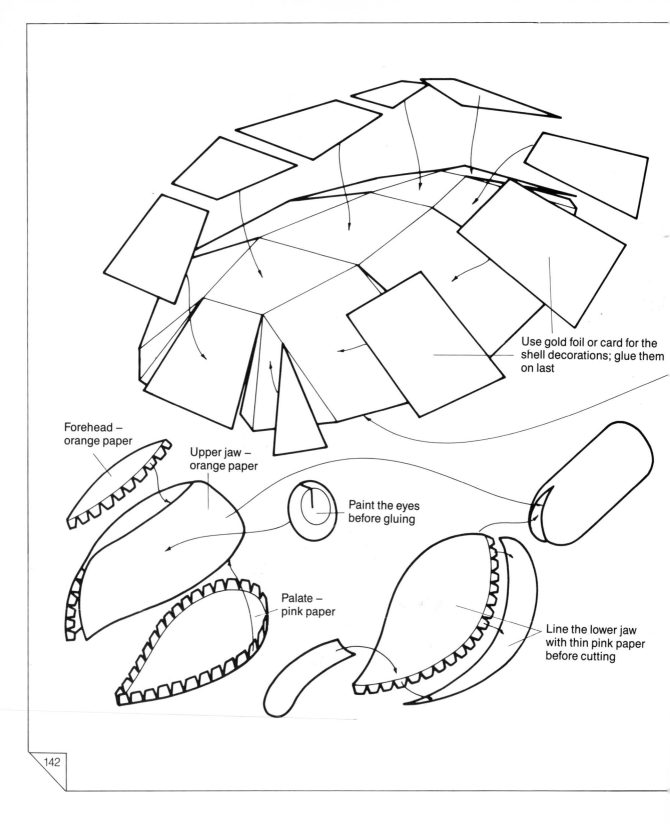

Use gold foil or card for the shell decorations; glue them on last

Forehead – orange paper

Upper jaw – orange paper

Paint the eyes before gluing

Palate – pink paper

Line the lower jaw with thin pink paper before cutting

142

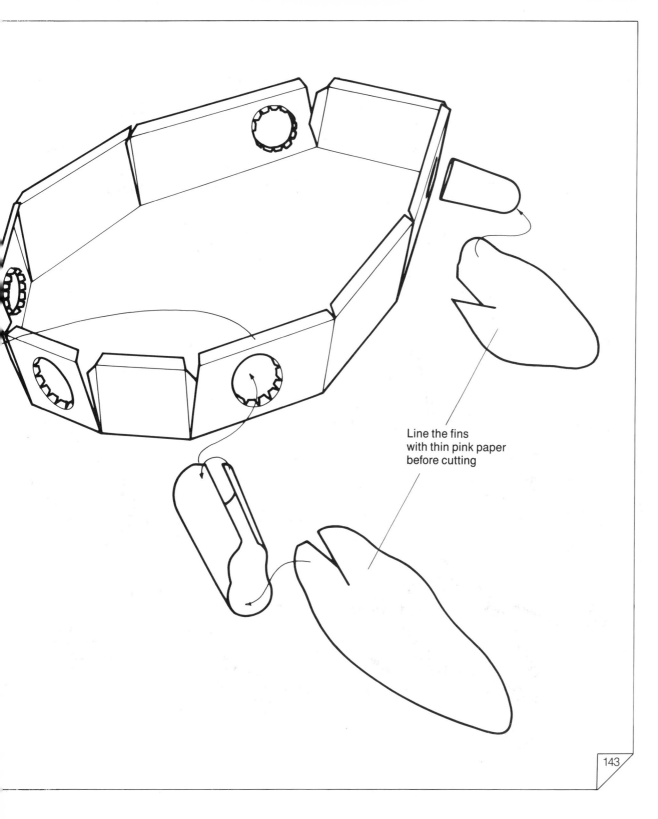

Line the fins
with thin pink paper
before cutting

INDEX

144

j 745.592
H 389 pap

CHICAGO HEIGHTS PUBLIC LIBRARY

CHICAGO HEIGHTS FREE LIBRARY

3 1539 00109 8441

96, 98, 00, 10

j-745.592
H389pap
Hawcock, David.
Paper dinosaurs: How to make 20 original
paper models.
c. 1

CHICAGO HEIGHTS FREE PUBLIC LIBRARY
15TH ST. & CHICAGO ROAD
CHICAGO HEIGHTS, ILL.
60411
PHONE: (708) 754-0323